The Holy Word for Morning Revival

Witness Lee

Living Stream Ministry
Anaheim, CA • www.lsm.org

First Edition, February 2011.

ISBN 978-0-7363-4743-3

Published by

Living Stream Ministry
2431 W. La Palma Ave., Anaheim, CA 92801 U.S.A.
P. O. Box 2121, Anaheim, CA 92814 U.S.A.

Printed in the United States of America

11 12 13 14 / 6 5 4 3 2 1

Contents

Preface

1. This book is intended as an aid to believers in developing a daily time of morning revival with the Lord in His word. At the same time, it provides a limited review of the International Chinese-speaking Conference held in Anaheim, California, February 18-20, 2011. The subject of the conference was "Speaking the Word of God." Through intimate contact with the Lord in His word, the believers can be constituted with life and truth and thereby equipped to prophesy in the meetings of the church unto the building up of the Body of Christ.

2. The content of this book is taken primarily from the conference message outlines, the text and footnotes of the Recovery Version of the Bible, selections from the writings of Witness Lee and Watchman Nee, and *Hymns,* all of which are published by Living Stream Ministry.

3. The book is divided into weeks. One conference message is covered per week. Each week presents first the message outline, followed by six daily portions, a hymn, and then some space for writing. The message outline has been divided into days, corresponding to the six daily portions. Each daily portion covers certain points and begins with a section entitled "Morning Nourishment." This section contains selected verses and a short reading that can provide rich spiritual nourishment through intimate fellowship with the Lord. The "Morning Nourishment" is followed by a section entitled "Today's Reading," a longer portion of ministry related to the day's main points. Each day's portion concludes with a short list of references for further reading and some space for the saints to make notes concerning their spiritual inspiration, enlightenment, and enjoyment to serve as a reminder of what they have received of the Lord that day.

4. The space provided at the end of each week is for composing a short prophecy. This prophecy can be composed by considering all of our daily notes, the "harvest" of our inspirations during the week, and preparing a main point

with some sub-points to be spoken in the church meetings for the organic building up of the Body of Christ.

5. Following the last week in this volume, we have provided reading schedules for both the Old and New Testaments in the Recovery Version with footnotes. These schedules are arranged so that one can read through both the Old and New Testaments of the Recovery Version with footnotes in two years.

6. As a practical aid to the saints' feeding on the Word throughout the day, we have provided verse cards at the end of the volume, which correspond to each day's scripture reading. These may be cut out and carried along as a source of spiritual enlightenment and nourishment in the saints' daily lives.

7. The conference outlines were compiled by Living Stream Ministry from the writings of Witness Lee and Watchman Nee. The outlines, footnotes, and references in the Recovery Version of the Bible are by Witness Lee. All of the other references cited in this publication are from the ministry of Witness Lee and Watchman Nee.

International Chinese-speaking Conference

(February 18-20, 2011)

General Subject:

Speaking the Word of God

Banners:

The speaking God, who created man in His image,
desires that man express Him and represent Him
by speaking for Him.

The beautifying function of the word of God is
for the church to be prepared to be Christ's glorious bride,
and the killing function of the word of God is
for the church to function as God's corporate warrior
in slaying His adversary.

We must live a proper, normal Christian life
—a prophesying life—
so that we may be the proper speaking ones
in the church meetings.

If we let the word of Christ dwell in us richly
and if we speak for God, the word of God
will grow, multiply, and prevail.

The Speaking God
Desiring That Man Speak for Him

Scripture Reading: Heb. 1:1-3; John 1:1, 14, 18; Gen. 1:26-28

Day 1 I. The Bible first reveals God, and second it reveals God's word; thus, in the Bible we first have God, and then we have God's speaking, the word that proceeds out of His mouth (Gen. 1:3; Heb. 1:1-2a; Matt. 4:4):

A. The center of reality in the universe is God, and the expression of God is the word; all the elements of God are in His word (Gen. 1:1, 3; John 1:1).

B. If God had not spoken anything, it would have been impossible for the universe to come into existence; our existence depends on God's speaking (Heb. 11:3; 2 Pet. 3:5; Psa. 33:6, 9; Gen. 1:26).

C. Our being saved and our receiving the eternal life are altogether dependent on God's speaking (1 Pet. 1:23, 25; John 5:24).

D. God has revealed Himself in His speaking; God is the revealed God because He has revealed Himself by speaking (Heb. 1:1-2a).

E. The Word of God is God Himself, for God and the Word are one; whenever we come to the Bible as the Word of God, we should come to God (John 1:1; 5:39-40; 2 Tim. 3:16).

Day 2 II. In the Godhead Christ is the Word (John 1:1):

A. Christ as the Word defines, explains, and expresses God; hence, Christ, as the Word, is the definition, explanation, and expression of God (v. 18).

B. This Word is actually God Himself, not God hidden, concealed, and mysterious but God defined, explained, and expressed (vv. 1, 14, 18).

C. The fact that the Word is the entire God means that the Word is for the speaking of the Triune God; the Word became incarnate as a man, and that man, Jesus Christ, was God's Word, God's speaking (vv. 1, 14; 6:63).

D. When Christ, the Word of God, was on earth speaking for God and teaching people, He did not speak from Himself; His teaching was not His own but was according to what the Father had taught Him (7:16; 8:28b; 12:49-50).

Day 3 III. **In His New Testament economy, the speaking God speaks in the Son (Heb. 1:1-2a):**
A. Today God does not speak to us in many portions or in many ways—God speaks to us in one person, the Son; God is now speaking in the Son, who is the Word of God (v. 2a; John 1:1, 14, 18).
B. The speaking Son, who is the Word of God and the speaking of God, is the Spirit (6:63; 1 Cor. 15:45b; 2 Cor. 3:17a):
  1. Whenever the Son speaks, He is the speaking Spirit (Rev. 2:1, 7a).
  2. God speaks in the Son, the Son as the speaking Spirit speaks to the churches, and ultimately the Spirit speaks with the church (22:17).
C. The Son upholds and bears all things by the word of His power; when He speaks, everything is in order (Heb. 1:3).

Day 4 D. Today the Son of God is no longer merely an individual; He is a corporate, universal man, the Body of Christ; for this reason, all the members of the Body can speak the word of God (1 Cor. 12:12; Eph. 5:30):
  1. God today continues to speak in His Son, who has been enlarged to become a corporate man, the Body of Christ (1 Cor. 12:12; Eph. 2:15; John 17:20).
  2. We are all members of the Body of Christ, God's Son; thus, when we speak, God is speaking in the Son (1 Cor. 12:12, 27; 2 Cor. 4:13; 5:20).
  3. As the firstborn Son of God being the Word of God is God's oracle for the speaking and dispensing of God to carry out His eternal economy, so the many sons of God being members of the Word of God are God's oracle speaking and

dispensing God for the spreading of God and the increase of Christ (John 1:1; Rom. 8:29; Heb. 2:10):

  a. The firstborn Son is the oracle of God, and we are the many sons; this means that all the sons are God's oracle so that God may have a spread and that Christ may have an increase (Acts 8:4; John 3:30, 34).

  b. Our speaking for God is for the fruit-bearing of God's multiplication and spreading (15:5).

Day 5 IV. **The speaking God desires that man speak for Him (Gen. 1:26):**

  A. God created man in His image so that man would express Him by speaking for Him (v. 26; 2:19-20):

    1. When God created man, the first marvelous thing was that He created a spirit within man, and the second was that man was given the ability to speak (vv. 7, 19-20).

    2. God created man in His image, and the most important aspect of God's image is that God speaks (1:26-27):

      a. Since God is a speaking God, when He created man in His image, He created man with the ability to speak (1 Cor. 2:13; 1 Thes. 2:2, 4).

      b. God created us not only to be like Him in having love, light, holiness, and righteousness but also in being able to speak (Gen. 1:26-27).

      c. Man's ability to speak is a manifestation of his likeness to God (v. 26a).

    3. God wants man to speak His word for His expression; God desires that we express Him mainly through our speaking for Him (2 Pet. 2:5; 1 Cor. 12:3).

Day 6 B. God created man to represent Him by speaking for Him (Gen. 1:26, 28):

    1. The most important requirement of a representative is that he must be able to speak; we

can represent God because we are able to speak
as God speaks (2 Cor. 5:19-20).

2. A representative should speak the words of the
   one he represents; as God's representatives,
   we represent God by speaking His words (John
   7:16-18; 12:49-50; Acts 4:29, 31; 13:44, 48-49;
   1 Thes. 2:13).

C. In order to speak for God, we need to have the full
   knowledge of the word of God, knowing the major
   items related to the word of God (1 Tim. 1:4; John
   1:1; 6:63; Eph. 6:18; Psa. 119:105; Matt. 4:4; 13:3;
   1 Pet. 1:23; Deut. 32:2; Heb. 4:12; Jer. 23:29).

Morning Nourishment

Heb. **By faith we understand that the universe has been**
11:3 **framed by the word of God, so that what is seen has**
not come into being out of things which appear.
Matt. **But He answered and said, It is written, "Man shall**
4:4 **not live on bread alone, but on every word that pro-**
ceeds out through the mouth of God."

The Bible first reveals God (Gen. 1:1). The whole universe is a mystery, and the center of this mystery is God. God created the heavens and the earth. Without God nothing would exist.

The second thing the Bible shows us is God's speaking, God's word. Hebrews 1:1-2a says, "God, having spoken of old in many portions and in many ways to the fathers in the prophets, has at the last of these days spoken to us in the Son." Thus, in the Bible we first have God, and then we have God's speaking, the word that proceeds out of His mouth. (*Life-study of Proverbs*, p. 39)

Today's Reading

All intellectuals acknowledge that human society is a mystery, that the universe is also a mystery, and that in this mystery there is a center of reality, which is God. The expression of this God is the word; all the elements of this God are in His word. Where there is God, there is the word. Where there is no God, there is no word.

We all acknowledge that God's creation of the universe was a great act. Yet this great act was accomplished by speaking. Genesis 1:3 says, "And God said, Let there be light; and there was light." Whatever God spoke came into existence. Therefore, in the Psalms the psalmist praised God, saying, "For He spoke, and it was; / He commanded, and it stood" (33:9). If God had not spoken anything, then it would have been impossible for the universe to come into existence. Even our existence depends to a great extent on God's speaking. The Lord Jesus said, "He who hears My word and believes...has eternal life" (John 5:24). Our being saved and our receiving the eternal life are altogether dependent upon the Lord's word. (*Speaking for God*, pp. 31, 35)

The book of Hebrews begins with God speaking. The divine

speaking is the opening point of this book. God has spoken! Praise Him! It is absolutely not a small thing that God has spoken. Without speaking God is mysterious. But He has revealed Himself in His speaking. He is no longer mysterious. Now He is the revealed God.

We need to consider this matter of God's speaking. If there were a God in the universe, what would be the first thing that He would do? Certainly, before doing anything else, He would speak. If God is living, He must certainly speak. If He is real, His speaking testifies His reality. If He is moving, He will move by speaking. If He is working, He will surely work by speaking. (*Life-study of Hebrews*, p. 17)

As the unique source, God is the Word. "In the beginning was the Word...and the Word was God" (John 1:1). Have you ever realized that the greatest wonder in the universe is the Word of God? Creation, redemption, regeneration, sanctification, and transformation all take place by the Word. If God had been silent—that is, if there had been no Word—there could have been no creation. Creation came about through God's speaking. When God spoke, all the items of creation came into being. How marvelous that our God is a speaking God! This speaking God is the Word. Regarding this, John 1:1 is a strategic verse, for this verse declares that the Word was God. (*The Secret of Experiencing Christ*, pp. 106-107)

In the Bible there is such a verse which says, "In the beginning was the Word, and the Word was with God, and the Word was God" (John 1:1). This is a great verse showing us that the Word and God are one. The Word is God, and God is the Word. Likewise, we can say that man is the word, and the word is man. Before this we might have never thought of ourselves as being the word. Although many animals can make certain vocal sounds, they cannot speak and do not have words. Only man has words; hence, man is the word. If someone wants to know what I am thinking within, he has to know it through my words. Therefore, when we come to the Bible, we come to God, because the Bible as the Word is God Himself. (*Speaking for God*, p. 34)

Further Reading: Speaking for God, ch. 2; *Life Messages*, vol. 1, ch. 24

Enlightenment and inspiration: _____

_____

_____

_____

Morning Nourishment

John In the beginning was the Word, and the Word was
1:1 with God, and the Word was God.
  14 ...The Word became flesh and tabernacled among us...
  18 No one has ever seen God; the only begotten Son, who
    is in the bosom of the Father, He has declared *Him*.

In the Godhead Christ is the Word. "In the beginning was the Word, and the Word was with God, and the Word was God" (John 1:1). The Word is the definition, explanation, and expression of God; hence, the Word is God defined, explained, and expressed.

God is mysterious. He needs the Word to express Him. Christ, as the Word, defines, explains, and expresses Him. Therefore, Christ, as the Word, is the definition, explanation, and expression of God. This Word is actually God Himself, not God hidden, concealed, and mysterious, but God defined, explained, and expressed. (*The Conclusion of the New Testament*, p. 235)

Today's Reading

The Word is eternal; that is, the Word is self-existing, without beginning. This is contrary to the heretical teaching that says the Word, the *Logos,* was created by God. According to the revelation in John's Gospel, the Word was not created. John 1:1 says that the Word was in the beginning. This reveals that the Word is eternal. This eternal Word is a living person, Christ, the Son of the living God (Rev. 19:13). Such a Word signifies the mysterious and invisible God defined and expressed.

This Word as the definition of the Triune God is for God's speaking. The fact that this Word is the entire God means that it is for the speaking of the Triune God. This Word became incarnate as a man, and that man was God's speaking. This means that the man Jesus Christ was God's Word, God's speaking. He spoke God not only with clear words but also with what He was and what He did. He is altogether the Word of God and the speaking of God. Sometimes He spoke with words, and at other times He spoke with actions. All that He was and all that He did spoke God.

John 1:14 says not only that the Word became flesh but also that the Word tabernacled among us...in order to declare God, express God, explain God, and define God in many practical ways. The incarnate Word is the speaking, the expression, and the definition of God. As the Word, Christ is the defined God, the explained, expressed, and revealed God, the God made known to human beings.

Christ is the expression of the Father. As the Son He is the issue, the coming out, of God, and He is also the expression of the Father. Because the Son expressed the Father, the Son is the expression of the Father.

Christ's being the Word is mainly to express God the Father by declaring, defining, and revealing Him (John 1:18). The more the Son speaks, the more God the Father is expressed.

In the Old Testament God spoke in the prophets, in men moved by His Spirit (Heb. 1:1; 2 Pet. 1:21). In the New Testament He speaks in the Son, who is God Himself expressed (Heb. 1:2-3). God the Father is hidden; God the Son is expressed. No one has ever seen God, but the Son as the Word of God, as the speaking of God, has declared and expressed Him. Whereas God spoke through the prophets in the Old Testament, He did not have Himself expressed. But in the New Testament God speaks in the Son, who expresses Him. Formerly God spoke through the prophets indirectly, but now He speaks directly in the Son, that is, in the One who is the expression of the Father. (*The Conclusion of the New Testament*, pp. 235-236)

Christ is the Word of God (John 1:1; Rev. 19:13) and the speaking of God (Heb. 1:2a). When He was on earth speaking for God and teaching people, His teaching was not His own but was according to what the Father had taught Him (John 7:16; 8:28b). He did not speak from Himself; as the Father spoke to Him, so He spoke (12:49-50). Today He is in us still speaking for God to reveal God and speaking God into people. (*Truth Lessons—Level Three*, vol. 2, p. 122)

Further Reading: Life-study of Hebrews, msg. 2; Crystallization-study of the Gospel of John, msg. 2

Enlightenment and inspiration: _____

_____

_____

_____

Morning Nourishment

Heb. God, having spoken of old in many portions and in
1:1-3 many ways to the fathers in the prophets, has at the
last of these days spoken to us in the Son...who, being
the effulgence of His glory and the impress of His substance and upholding and bearing all things by the
word of His power, having made purification of sins,
sat down on the right hand of the Majesty on high.

Without God, the universe is a tragedy, and without the speaking of God, we would be in misery. But, hallelujah, we have God,
and we have God's speaking.

God has spoken, and today God still speaks. There are many
matters in God's speaking. For instance, Hebrews 1:1-2 says, "God,
having spoken of old in many portions and in many ways to the
fathers in the prophets, has at the last of these days spoken to us
in the Son, whom He appointed Heir of all things, through whom
also He made the universe." Today God speaks to us in the Son.
He does not speak to us in many portions or in many ways, or
through the prophets, but in the Son. He speaks to us in one person, the Son. (*The Apostles' Teaching*, p. 9)

Today's Reading

A literal rendering of the Greek would read, "God...has...spoken
to us in Son." Darby had a marvelous realization. He said that since
there is no article, it must mean that God speaks in the person of
the Son. There is only one God (Isa. 45:5; 1 Cor. 8:4), and the name
of our God is the Father, the Son, and the Spirit (Matt. 28:19). This
is similar to the practice in many societies of naming one person
with three names, first, middle, and last. This is quite meaningful.
M. R. Vincent indicated in his writing that a name always denotes
a person. Thus, God's speaking "in Son" means that God speaks in
the person of the Son. (*The Apostles' Teaching*, p. 10)

Whenever the Son speaks, He is the Spirit. The speaking Son
is the Spirit. The Son of God is the Word. When the Word voices, it
becomes the Spirit. This is proved by the seven epistles in Revelation 2 and 3. At the beginning of each epistle, it says that the Lord

is speaking, but at the end it says that we should hear what the Spirit is saying to the churches. This proves that whenever the Lord Jesus speaks, He is the speaking Spirit. Whenever the Son is speaking, it is the Spirit speaking. If you consider the seven comparisons in Revelation 2 and 3, you will see that whatever the Son speaks is the speaking of the Spirit (Rev. 2:1 cf. 7; 2:8 cf. 11; 2:12 cf. 17; 2:18 cf. 29; 3:1 cf. 6; 3:7 cf. 13; 3:14 cf. 22). We have the Son who is the Word of God. He is not only the Word of God but also the speaking of God. Whenever He speaks, He is the speaking Spirit. "The words which I have spoken to you are spirit and are life" (John 6:63).

Today the Son as the speaking Spirit is speaking with the churches. He not only speaks to the churches but also with the churches. Revelation 22:17 says, "And the Spirit and the bride say, Come!" At the beginning of the book of Revelation it is the Spirit speaking to the churches, but at the end of Revelation it is the Spirit speaking with the churches because the speaking Spirit and the church have become one. Hallelujah! This is God's speaking. (*Life-study of Hebrews*, p. 29)

The Greek word [for *word* in Hebrews 1:3] denotes the instant word. The Son upholds and bears all things not by His work but by His instant word, the word of His power. In creation all things came into being through Him as the Word (John 1:1-3). The universe has been framed by the word of God (Heb. 11:3): "He spoke, and it was; He commanded, and it stood" (Psa. 33:9). In salvation we are saved through His word (John 5:24; Rom. 10:8, 17). It is through His word that His authority with power is exercised (Matt. 8:8-9). It is by His word that His healing power is realized (John 4:50-51). Here, this book says that God speaks in the Son and the Son upholds and bears all things by His word. It is altogether a matter of speaking. When the Lord speaks, everything is in order. (Heb. 1:3, footnote 2)

Further Reading: Life-study of Hebrews, msg. 3; *The Apostles' Teaching,* ch. 1

Enlightenment and inspiration: _____

_____

_____

_____

Morning Nourishment

John For He whom God has sent speaks the words of God,
3:34 for He gives the Spirit not by measure.
2 Cor. And having the same spirit of faith according to that
4:13 which is written, "I believed, therefore I spoke," we
also believe, therefore we also speak.

Before His crucifixion and resurrection, the Lord Jesus was restricted by the flesh. It was not possible for Him to be universal. But through death and resurrection He was enlarged from an individual to a corporate man. On the day of Pentecost Christ came down as the all-inclusive Spirit upon His disciples to make them members of His Body. This Body, a corporate man, includes the resurrected Christ as the Head and the millions of believers in Christ as the members. Now, just as my whole body speaks whenever I speak, so the Body of Christ speaks whenever Christ speaks as the Head. Today the Son of God is no longer merely an individual; He is a corporate, universal man. For this reason, all the members of the Body can speak the word of God. Even young people can go to their parents or classmates and speak to them on God's behalf. (*Life-study of Colossians*, p. 568)

Today's Reading

We all were saved through the hearing of God's word. When I was saved in China more than fifty years ago, God Himself did not come to speak to me directly. Rather, I heard God's word through a member of His Body. This is one example of the fact that God today continues to speak in His Son who has been enlarged to become a corporate man, the Body of Christ. How wonderful that we all are part of the enlargement of Christ, part of a universal man of which Christ is the Head and we are the members! (*Life-study of Colossians*, pp. 568-569)

As the firstborn Son of God being the Word of God (John 1:1) is God's oracle for the speaking and dispensing of God to carry out His eternal economy, so the many sons of God being members of the Word of God are God's oracle speaking and dispensing God for the spreading of God and the increase of Christ. The firstborn Son of God is the oracle of God, and we are the many sons. This means that all the sons are God's oracle so that God may have a spread and Christ may have an increase.

The constituents of the vital groups are also the prophets of God (1 Cor. 14:1, 31). Since all the sons of God are God's oracle, they become God's prophets, the ones who speak God, speak for God, and speak forth God. A prophet is a speaking one. The Greek word for *prophesy* means to speak for or speak forth.

We are the members of Christ, constituting an organism for His increase through His multiplication (Rom. 12:5; John 15:5). Because we are Christ's members, we are a part of Him. We are members of Christ, not individualistically, but corporately.... Christ must be multiplied so that He can have an increase. In John 3 the bride is the increase of the Bridegroom (vv. 29-30), just as Eve was the increase of Adam.

We are His brothers participating with Him in the divine sonship with the divine right to express God mainly through speaking for the dispensing of God through His oracle (Rom. 8:29; Heb. 1:2). The Lord Jesus was with the disciples for three and a half years, but He never called them His brothers until after His resurrection. When He resurrected, He told Mary, "Go to My brothers and say to them, I ascend to My Father and your Father, and My God and your God" (John 20:17). Through regeneration in resurrection, we all became His brothers (1 Pet. 1:3). His resurrection was a great delivery of Himself as the firstborn Son of God and of us as His many brothers, the many sons of God. We are His brothers, sharing in His divine sonship.

In God's oracle we become the prophets of God speaking God, speaking for God, and speaking forth God (1 Cor. 14:1, 31).

Our speaking for God is for the fruit-bearing of God's multiplication and spreading (John 15:5). A tree multiplies and spreads by bearing fruit. (*The Vital Groups*, pp. 28, 37-38)

Further Reading: Life-study of Colossians, msg. 64; *The Vital Groups,* msgs. 3-4

Enlightenment and inspiration: _____

_____

_____

_____

Morning Nourishment

1 Cor. ...We speak, not in words taught by human wisdom
2:13 but in words taught by the Spirit, interpreting spiritual things with spiritual *words.*

1 Thes. But even as we have been approved by God to be en-
2:4 trusted with the gospel, so we speak, not as pleasing men but God, who proves our hearts.

God is a speaking God. He created the universe and continues to do all things through His speaking. Therefore, everyone who has been saved and who has His life should learn to speak for Him and to speak His word.

The greatest mystery in the universe is God....This mystery is opened and revealed to us in His Word. Hebrews 1 tells us that our God is a speaking God (vv. 1-2). The speaking of the human race came from His creation. He is a speaking God, and He is also the Word. (*Speaking for God,* p. 41)

Today's Reading

God's desire...is that man speak for Him. This matter sounds easy to understand, but it contains a biblical mystery. God shows us clearly in the Bible that His purpose in creating man was that man might speak for Him. Genesis 1:26 says, "God said, Let Us make man in Our image, according to Our likeness." This was spoken during a council of the Divine Trinity to determine how to create man. The result was that God made man in His image.

Another special matter in God's creation of man is that since God is a speaking God, when He created man in His image, He created man with the ability to speak just like Himself. Because God is a God of love, light, holiness, and righteousness, He created man with love, light, holiness and righteousness. Because God is a speaking God, He created man to be...able to speak.

Inwardly in our image we are like God, having love, light, holiness, and righteousness. Outwardly, God is a speaking God, and like Him, we also are able to speak. Among God's creatures, there are only two kinds that can speak. One kind consists of the angels in heaven. Angels do speak. Before the Lord Jesus was born, an angel came to reveal His name to Joseph (Matt. 1:20-21). Charles Wesley wrote a hymn: "Hark! the herald angels sing, / 'Glory to the new-born King'" (*Hymns,* #84). Therefore, it was an angel who spoke first, and it was an angel who announced the good news first [Luke 2:10]; thereafter, we must preach the gospel.

We have already pointed out that God created man with two outstanding features: one is that He created a spirit within man, and the other is that He created a speaking organ for man.

The purpose of God in creating man in His image was that man might express Him. In which points does man express Him? First, man expresses Him in speaking. There are some Christians today who believe that we can express God by our behavior alone and without speaking. In other words, they say that if we have a good testimony and a proper living with good behavior, we will be able to express God in the presence of men. This is not wrong, and this has its place, but we cannot avoid the matter of speaking for God. Speaking cannot be replaced; speaking is the real expression. Suppose there is a preacher who dresses himself tidily and properly and has his hair combed neatly, and when he stands on the podium, he is gentle and courteous, giving people the feeling that he really behaves well. However, if he would stand there for two hours, staring at the congregation with a smile but without saying a word, the congregation would not be satisfied, and he would not be able to express God. Therefore, when we express God, we need to have a proper living, but even more we need to speak forth clear words.

God wants us to express Him mainly through our speaking for Him. In the time of Noah when the whole earth was corrupted, God came and called Noah to be a herald of righteousness (2 Pet. 2:5), and Noah then preached the righteous words of God for one hundred and twenty years. Today we should speak for God in the same way. (*Speaking for God,* pp. 41-45, 54-55)

Further Reading: The Practice of the Church Life according to the God-ordained Way, ch. 4; Life-study of 1 Corinthians, msg. 57

Enlightenment and inspiration: _____

_____

_____

_____

Morning Nourishment

John ...I have not spoken from Myself; but the Father who
12:49-50 sent Me, He Himself has given Me commandment, what
to say and what to speak. And I know that His commandment is eternal life. The things therefore that I
speak, even as the Father has said to Me, so I speak.

God is a speaking God, and when He created us, He wanted us
also to speak....According to Genesis 1:26, God created us not only
that we might have His image but even more that we might rule
for Him. Therefore, He gave us the authority to have dominion over
all the other creatures, that is, "over the fish of the sea and over
the birds of heaven and over the cattle and over all the earth."

Human beings are able to speak...because we are God's representatives. He created us that we might represent Him. The most
important requirement of a representative is that he must be
able to speak. If today someone sends a representative to us, yet
this representative, being dumb, is not able to talk, then in the
end no agreement can be reached since there is no possibility of
having any discussion. This kind of representative is a useless
representative. Today we can represent God because we can
speak. (*Speaking for God*, pp. 44-45)

Today's Reading

We need to know what kinds of words God wanted man to
speak when He created man with the ability to speak. Did He
want man merely to speak the words of man? God created man to
represent Him. A representative should speak the words of the
one he represents. As God's representatives,...we must speak God's
words. We have to speak for God and speak forth God; this God is
the word.

Since we all have been begotten of God, within us we ought to
have the "God language"; whatever we speak, we speak God. In
America there are people of different colors: white, red, yellow,
brown, and black. Among these races, the different Asian peoples
are difficult to distinguish outwardly. For example, the Chinese and
the Koreans look very much alike....How then does one tell the

difference? It is by listening to their speech. Once they begin to talk, we know then that this one is Chinese and that one is Korean. ...We speak the words of the one of whom we were born. Since we were born of God, naturally we speak God's words. Since God's word is God Himself, when we speak God's word, we speak God.

Although we became fallen, once we are regenerated and our spirit is made alive, we are doubly able to speak for God, even more able than Adam. Adam was only created, not regenerated. Although we were created and became fallen, we have been regenerated and saved. John 1:12-13 says, "But as many as received Him, to them He gave the authority to become children of God, to those who believe into His name, who were begotten not of blood, nor of the will of the flesh, nor of the will of man, but of God." Since we have been begotten of God, we can speak the word of God. If a child is born of us and is not dumb, it is impossible for him to be unable to speak human words. Therefore, we all need to be encouraged to speak the word of God after our regeneration.

How do we speak for God? To speak for God, we need to have the full knowledge of the word of God (1 Tim. 2:4). Today the main reason that Christians cannot speak for God is that they do not understand the word of God. Therefore, we need to learn to understand the word of God; then we will be able to speak for God.

For us to live a normal life today, we must be in the word of God. ...For the church to be strong and normal, built up, spiritual, and mature in life, we must speak the word of God. What we need today is our God, who is the word. This word is in the Holy Scriptures. We must receive the word and speak the word. Thus, the word of God as Christ, as the Spirit, as life, as light, as food, as the seed, as the rain, as the dew, as a sword, and as a hammer will be manifested as a reality upon us. The word of God can do innumerable things; everything hinges on God's word. Hence, we must do all we can to read the Word of God. (*Speaking for God*, pp. 47-48, 55-56, 39)

Further Reading: Speaking for God, ch. 3; The Ministry of God's Word, ch. 1

Enlightenment and inspiration: _____

_____

_____

_____

Hymns, #903

1 Lord, speak to me, that I may speak
   In living echoes of Thy tone;
   As Thou hast sought, so let me seek
   Thy erring children lost and lone.

2 O lead me, Lord, that I may lead
   The wandering and the wavering feet;
   O feed me, Lord, that I may feed
   Thy hungering ones with manna sweet.

3 O strengthen me, that while I stand
   Firm on the rock, and strong in Thee,
   I may stretch out a loving hand
   To wrestlers with the troubled sea.

4 O teach me, Lord, that I may teach
   The precious things Thou dost impart;
   And wing my words, that they may reach
   The hidden depths of many a heart.

5 O give Thine own sweet rest to me,
   That I may speak with soothing power
   A word in season, as from Thee
   To weary ones in needful hour.

6 O fill me with Thy fulness, Lord,
   Until my very heart o'erflow
   In kindling thought and glowing word,
   Thy love to tell, Thy praise to show.

7 O use me, Lord, use even me,
   Just as Thou wilt, and when, and where,
   Until Thy blessed face I see,
   Thy rest, Thy joy, Thy glory share!

Composition for prophecy with main point and sub-points: _____

_____

_____

_____

_____

_____

_____

_____

_____

_____

_____

_____

_____

_____

_____

_____

_____

_____

_____

_____

_____

_____

_____

_____

_____

_____

_____

_____

_____

_____

_____

_____

*The Beautifying and Killing Functions
of the Word of God for the Church
as the Glorious Bride of Christ
and the Corporate Warrior of God*

Scripture Reading: Eph. 5:26-27; 6:17-18; Rev. 19:7-9, 11-16

Day 1 I. **The beautifying function of the word of God is for the church to be prepared to be Christ's glorious bride, and the killing function of the word of God is for the church to function as God's corporate warrior in slaying His adversary (Eph. 5:26-27; 6:17-18; Rev. 19:7-9, 11-16):**

A. In Ephesians 5 the word is for nourishment that leads to the beautifying of the bride, but in Ephesians 6 the word is for killing that enables the church as the corporate warrior to engage in spiritual warfare.

B. The beautifying function of the word of God produces the church in the image of God, and the killing function of the word of God issues in the church with the dominion of God (Gen. 1:26).

C. The overcomers live by every word that proceeds out through the mouth of God in order to be governed, controlled, ruled, and restricted by the Word of God in following Him to become His bride for His expression and to defeat His enemy for His dominion (Matt. 4:4; Deut. 17:18-20; Rev. 19:13-14).

D. The Lord Jesus came as the Word of God in the flesh to judicially redeem the church (John 1:14), He became the life-giving Spirit as the word of God to organically save the church (1 Cor. 15:45b; Eph. 5:26; 6:17), and He will return as the Word of God with His overcomers to set up His kingdom on earth (Rev. 19:13-16; 17:14; Dan. 2:34-35, 44-45).

II. **As the bride, the church must be beautiful, "not having spot or wrinkle or any such things"; the beautifying of the church is by Christ as**

the life-giving Spirit sanctifying the church,
cleansing her by the washing (lit., laver) of the
water in the word (Eph. 5:26-27):

A. The beauty of the bride comes from the very
   Christ who is wrought into the church and who
   is then expressed through the church; our only
   beauty is the reflection of Christ, the shining out
   of Christ from within us (2 Cor. 3:16-18).

Day 2
&
Day 3

B. In the past, Christ as the Redeemer gave Himself
   up for the church (Eph. 5:25) for redemption and the
   impartation of life (John 19:34); in the present, He
   as the life-giving Spirit is sanctifying the church,
   beautifying her, by the washing (the laver) of the
   water in the word; and in the future, He as the
   Bridegroom will present the church to Himself as
   His counterpart for His satisfaction (Eph. 5:26-27;
   cf. S. S. 8:13-14).

C. Unless the priests in the tabernacle washed in
   the laver, there was no way for the tabernacle to
   operate; likewise, unless we are cleansed by the
   laver of the water in the word from earthly defilement, there is no way for the church life to operate (Exo. 30:17-21; Eph. 5:26).

D. The Bible speaks of two kinds of defilement: the
   defilement that comes from sin and the defilement
   that comes from the earthly touch, from having
   contact with the things of the world (cf. John
   13:12-17).

E. The washing at the laver signifies not the washing away of sin by the blood of Christ but the
   washing away of the defilement that comes from
   contacting earthly things, by the life-giving, speaking Spirit:

   1. The life-giving Spirit is the speaking Spirit,
      and whatever He speaks instantly and pres-
      ently (Gk. *rhema*) is the word that washes us.

   2. The way to have the washing of the water in the
      word is to pray-read the Word (Eph. 6:17-18).

   3. If day by day there is no speaking of the Lord

within us, then in our practical experience the Spirit is absent, for the Lord's speaking actually is the Spirit (John 6:63; Eph. 6:17).

4. As long as we have the Lord's present word, we have the life-giving Spirit; we know that Christ as our person is present with us by His speaking, for His speaking is the very presence of the life-giving Spirit.

Day 4

F. The laver typifies the washing power of the life-giving Spirit issuing from the death of Christ; the locating of the laver after the altar signifies that the washing power of the laver comes out of God's judgment at the altar:

1. After passing through God's full judgment at the altar (the cross), the crucified Christ entered into resurrection and became the life-giving Spirit who washes us (1 Cor. 15:45; 6:11; Titus 3:5).

2. The dimensions of the laver are not given, signifying that the life-giving Spirit is immeasurable, unlimited (John 3:34).

G. The laver was made of bronze from the mirrors of the serving women who served at the entrance of the Tent of Meeting (Exo. 38:8):

1. Bronze signifies God's righteous judgment (cf. Num. 16:38-39; 21:9).

2. The laver of bronze was a mirror that could reflect and expose, indicating that the word of Christ has the power to expose and judge our uncleanness and show our need to be washed.

Day 5

III. We need to "receive the...sword of the Spirit, which Spirit is the word of God, by means of all prayer and petition, praying at every time in spirit" (Eph. 6:17-18a):

A. The antecedent of *which* is *Spirit*, not *sword*, indicating that the Spirit is the word of God; both the Spirit and the word are Christ (2 Cor. 3:17; Rev. 19:13).

B. Christ as the Spirit and the word furnishes us

with a sword as an offensive weapon to defeat and slay the adversary.

C. The sword, the Spirit, and the word are one; when the constant word in the Bible becomes the instant word, that word is the Spirit as the sword that kills the adversary.

Day 6

D. We should pray-read the Word primarily to experience the sword as the killing instrument to slay God's adversary; since the enemy has injected himself into our being, what we need is for the killing power of the word to be applied to us to deal with the elements of the adversary within us (Eph. 6:17-18).

E. Pray-reading is a practical way to kill the negative elements within us.

F. Because the self is the greatest enemy, we need to experience the killing power of God's word; the more we take in the word with its killing power, the more our pride and all the negative elements within us are put to death.

G. As we pray-read the Word, the battle is raging as the negative elements in our being are slain; eventually, the self, the worst foe of all, will be put to death.

Morning Nourishment

Eph. **That He might sanctify her, cleansing *her* by the**
5:26-27 **washing of the water in the word, that He might pre-**
sent the church to Himself glorious, not having spot
or wrinkle or any such things, but that she would be
holy and without blemish.
6:17-18 **And receive...the sword of the Spirit, which *Spirit* is**
the word of God, by means of all prayer and petition,
praying at every time in spirit...

Pray-reading is the way to kill the adversary within us. Every day and in every kind of situation, you should pray-read. Whenever you are troubled by something negative within you, take the word of God by means of prayer in spirit. As you do this, the negative element will be killed.

In Ephesians 5 the word is for nourishment that leads to the beautifying of the bride. But in Ephesians 6 the word is for killing that enables the church as the corporate warrior to engage in spiritual warfare. Through the killing word, the adversary within us is slain. Sometimes we gain the victory over the enemy objectively, but we are defeated by the adversary subjectively. Although we may rejoice that the enemy outwardly is fleeing, we are still troubled by the adversary within us who remains. For this reason, we should be more concerned for the hidden adversary within us. Let us kill the adversary by pray-reading the word. (*Life-study of Ephesians,* pp. 821-822)

Today's Reading

Christ is now preparing us to be His bride. The time is coming when He will present the bride to Himself. Surely at the time of her presentation to Christ, the bride will not have any wrinkles or spots. In His bride Christ will behold nothing but beauty. This beauty will be the reflection of what He is....The beauty of the bride...comes from the very Christ who is wrought into the church and who is then expressed through the church. Our beauty is not our behavior. Our only beauty is the reflection of Christ, the shining out of Christ from within us. What Christ appreciates in us is the expression of Himself in us. Nothing less than this will meet His standard or win His appreciation.

Firstly, Christ must come into us and then be assimilated by us. Then He will be able to shine out of us. This shining is the glory of the bride, the manifestation of divinity through humanity. Real beauty is the expression of the divine attributes through humanity. Nothing in the universe is as beautiful as this expression. Therefore, the beauty of the bride is Christ shining out of us. It is a matter of divinity expressed through humanity. Through our humanity there is an expression of the divine color, the divine appearance, the divine flavor, the divine nature, and the divine character. Hallelujah for such a beauty!

On the day of his wedding, a bridegroom cares much more for the beauty of his bride than for her ability. In like manner,...the Lord Jesus cares much more for our beauty than for our function. Do not pay that much attention to becoming capable, qualified, and gifted in function....Eventually the Lord will show us that what He cares for is not our ability; He cares for the beauty of Himself expressed through our humanity. Christ does not intend to present a capable church to Himself. The church that will be presented to Him will be glorious and beautiful, a church without spot, wrinkle, or any such thing. If our blemishes and imperfections are to be removed, we need to take in more and more of Christ. He should not simply energize us for our function but also beautify us that we may be His bride.

At the time of the wedding, what the church will need is beauty, not strength. Oh, the church is being beautified by partaking of Christ, by digesting Christ, and by assimilating Christ! The more we experience the indwelling Christ in this way, the more He will replace our spots and wrinkles with His element, and the more His riches with the divine attributes will become our beauty. Then we shall be prepared to be presented to Christ as His lovely bride. (*Life-study of Ephesians*, pp. 800-801)

Further Reading: Life-study of Ephesians, msgs. 71, 95

Enlightenment and inspiration: _____

_____

_____

_____

Morning Nourishment

Eph. 5:25-27 ...Christ also loved the church and gave Himself up for her that He might sanctify her, cleansing *her* by the washing of the water in the word, that He might present the church to Himself glorious, not having spot or wrinkle or any such things, but that she would be holy and without blemish.

Ephesians 5:25-27 presents Christ to us in three stages. Verse 25 says that Christ loved the church and gave Himself up for her. Here we see Christ in the stage of the flesh. Verse 26 speaks of Christ sanctifying the church, cleansing her by the washing of the water in the word. In this verse we have Christ in the stage of the life-giving Spirit. Finally, a third stage of Christ is revealed in verse 27, which speaks of Christ presenting the church to Himself in His coming back. Hence, in this stage Christ will be the Bridegroom receiving His bride. The first of these three stages was in the past, the second is in the present, and the third will be in the future. In the first stage Christ was the Redeemer; in the second, He is the life-giving Spirit; and in the third, He will be the Bridegroom. (*Life-study of Ephesians*, p. 463)

Today's Reading

It was in the flesh that the Lord gave Himself up for us. If He had not given Himself up as a man in the flesh, there would have been no way for us to gain Him....According to Hebrews 2, Christ did not take on the nature of angels, but He did take on blood and flesh. Furthermore, John 1 says that the Word which was God and was with God became flesh (v. 14). Great is the mystery of godliness—God was manifest in the flesh (1 Tim. 3:16). God cannot be manifest in angels; He can be manifest only in the flesh.

If Christ had not put on human nature, it would be impossible for us to receive Him into us. The very Christ we take as our person is the God-man. It is impossible for us to take in God directly. Only after God has become the God-man can we take Him into our being to be our life and our person.

After the Lord Jesus gave Himself for us in the flesh, He was resurrected and in resurrection became the life-giving Spirit (1 Cor. 15:45). As the life-giving Spirit, He is the speaking Spirit. Whatever He speaks is the word that washes us. The Greek word rendered *word* in Ephesians 5:26 is not *logos*, the constant word, but *rhema*, which denotes the instant word, the word the Lord presently speaks to us. As the life-giving Spirit, the Lord is not silent; He is constantly speaking. If you take Him as your person, you will discover how much He desires to speak within you. Idols are dumb, but the indwelling Christ is always speaking. No one who takes Christ as his life and his person can remain silent. On the contrary, he will be constrained by Christ to speak.

If there is no speaking, no *rhema*, then in our practical experience the Spirit is absent, for the Lord's speaking actually is the Spirit. As long as we have the Lord's present word, we have the Spirit, the life-giving Spirit. We cannot separate Christ as the life-giving Spirit from His speaking. His presence consists in His speaking....If we do not have His speaking within us, we do not have His presence. But if we turn to Him to mean business to take Christ as our life and our person, His speaking will begin again. His speaking is the living word, the living word is the Spirit, and the Spirit is our wonderful Christ Himself. How practical, subjective, intimate, and real He is as the speaking Spirit!

Through the Lord's speaking within us as the life-giving Spirit, we are becoming a glorious church, a church holy and without blemish. Today we are waiting for the Lord's coming back, knowing that when He comes, He will present us to Himself a glorious church, holy and without blemish. At that time, we shall experience Christ in the third stage as the Bridegroom coming for His bride. Until then, our need is to daily take Christ as our person and to be cleansed, purified, and sanctified through the speaking of the life-giving Spirit. In this way we shall undergo a metabolic change leading to the transformation in life which is necessary for the church life. (*Life-study of Ephesians*, pp. 463-466, 469)

Further Reading: Life-study of Ephesians, msgs. 54-55

Enlightenment and inspiration: _____

_____

_____

_____

Morning Nourishment

Exo.   You shall also make a laver of bronze...for washing....
30:18-21   And Aaron and his sons shall wash their hands and
their feet *with water* from it; when they go into the
Tent of Meeting, they shall wash with water, that they
may not die; or when they come near to the altar to
minister, to burn an offering by fire to Jehovah, they
shall wash their hands and their feet, that they may
not die...

The laver is for the tabernacle's operation. In the outer court
there were the altar and the laver; in the Holy Place, the table, the
lampstand, and the incense altar; and in the Holy of Holies, the
ark....Without the laver, nothing in the tabernacle or in the outer
court could operate. For the operation of the tabernacle it was necessary for sacrifices to be offered at the altar....It was also necessary for the priests to come into the Holy Place to arrange the
bread on the table and trim the lamps...[and] intercede at the
incense altar. All this is involved in the operation of the tabernacle. Whenever the priests were to come to the altar to offer something to God or were to come into the tabernacle to serve, they
first had to go to the laver to wash their hands. Unless the priests
washed in the laver, there was no way for the tabernacle to operate....If the laver were removed from the outer court, everything
else in the tabernacle and outer court would still be complete.
However, there would not be any way for those things to operate.
(*Life-study of Exodus*, pp. 1669-1670)

Today's Reading

The service of the priests in the outer court and in the tabernacle depended on their washing in the laver....To confess our sins
to the Lord is to experience one kind of washing. However, this is
the washing by the blood, not the washing by the water in the
laver. In order to wash away our sin, sins, trespasses, and trans-
gressions, we need the blood. We also need the blood to wash us of
our mistakes, failures, defects, defeats, and shortcomings....How-
ever, when the Lord Jesus washed His disciples' feet, He used

water. That kind of washing did not require blood. The feet of the disciples were dirty and needed to be washed with water. The problem was not one of sin, but of dirt, of defilement.

The Bible...speaks of two kinds of defilement: the defilement that comes from sin and the defilement that comes by the earthly touch.... We may be defiled...by having contact with the things of the world.

I always wash my hands before eating because I realize that on this earth there is dirt everywhere. Our hands may become dirty even by touching our clothing. In the same principle, we can easily be defiled spiritually by having contact with earthly things. Simply by living and walking on this earth, we become defiled.

When we pray to offer something to the Lord, we first need to wash our hands and even our feet in the laver. To come to the meeting to function is actually to come into the tabernacle to serve the Lord. Before we serve the Lord in the tabernacle, we need to wash. However, in the Christian life of many believers and in their service to God there does not seem to be a laver. When they come to the altar to make an offering to God, they have unclean hands. They may come into the church meetings and serve without washing their hands in the laver. This kind of service brings in death. This is the reason Exodus 30:21 says, "They shall wash their hands and their feet, that they may not die."

We should be careful not to touch God's service unless we have first washed our hands in the laver. If we try to serve God in the tabernacle with unclean hands, we shall die, spiritually speaking. How much death there is among Christians today! The more they serve, the more death they have because they serve with unclean hands. Praying and serving with unclean hands brings in death.

If we do not pray in the meetings or function, in a sense we may be somewhat living. But if we pray or function without washing in the laver, we shall bring death to ourselves and also spread death to others. Death is the result of our trying to pray or serve without washing in the laver. (*Life-study of Exodus*, pp. 1670-1673)

Further Reading: Life-study of Exodus, msg. 156

Enlightenment and inspiration: _____

_____

_____

_____

Morning Nourishment

Titus Not out of works in righteousness which we did but
3:5   according to His mercy He saved us, through the
       washing of regeneration and the renewing of the
       Holy Spirit.
Exo.   And he made the laver of bronze and its base of
38:8   bronze from the mirrors of the serving women who
       served at the entrance of the Tent of Meeting.

In location the laver is after the altar, but in function the laver is before the altar. When the priests came to minister at the altar, they first had to wash at the laver. They also had to wash at the laver before going into the tabernacle to minister.

The location of the laver indicates that it comes out of the altar. The altar was overlaid with bronze, and the laver was made of bronze. In typology bronze signifies God's judgment. The altar typifies the cross of Christ. At the altar, at the cross, God's judgment was exercised to the fullest extent. Out of the judgment of God exercised at the altar, the laver was produced. The bronze on the altar signifies judgment, but the bronze on the laver signifies the result, the issue, of God's judgment....The washing power of the laver comes out of God's judgment.

Titus 3:5 speaks of the washing of regeneration and the renewing of the Holy Spirit. This verse reveals that the life-giving Spirit, the Spirit of life, is the washing power. Hence, the laver signifies the washing through the life-giving Spirit.

The laver typifies the washing power of the life-giving Spirit brought forth by the death of Christ. The altar signifies Christ's redemption, and the laver signifies the life-giving Spirit's washing....The life-giving Spirit is actually Christ Himself. After passing through God's full judgment and entering into resurrection, the crucified Christ became the life-giving Spirit who washes us. (*Life-study of Exodus*, pp. 1673-1674)

Today's Reading

The bronze used to overlay the altar came from the censers of the two hundred fifty rebellious ones who were judged by God...

(Num. 16:37-38)....Therefore, the bronze used to overlay the altar became a reminder of God's judgment on rebellion.

The bronze on the laver came from the looking glasses of the women who assembled at the door of the tent of meeting (Exo. 38:8)....This implies that the laver of bronze was a looking glass, a mirror, that could reflect and expose. Whereas the bronze on the altar was a reminder of God's judgment, the bronze on the laver was a mirror to expose God's people. It indicates that the judgment suffered by Christ on the cross has the power to expose us.

Those who came to the laver had their uncleanness exposed. In this way they would realize their need to wash....The bronze of the laver is a mirror reflecting our condition and exposing our dirt.

At the laver we have the bronze, the mirror, and the water. When we are at the laver, the bronze should remind us that whatever is sinful, earthly, and fleshly has been judged by God on the cross. But although we may confess our sins, we may not realize how much we are still worldly and fleshly. In the sight of God we have been redeemed, but we still need to be washed. Having been redeemed by the blood at the altar, we need to be washed by the water in the laver.

The more we walk in the Spirit and live in the mingled spirit, the more we shall be washed. Each washing will be a reminder not to go to certain places, contact certain persons, or be involved in situations that will defile us. Even though we may not do anything sinful, we may touch something worldly and natural and thereby be defiled. If we remain in a condition of defilement, we shall not be able to pray, serve the Lord, or function in the meetings. If we try to function without washing away the defilement in the laver, we shall experience death.

Exodus 30:19 [says], "And Aaron and his sons shall wash their hands and their feet with water from it."...This washing signifies the washing away of the defilement that comes from the earthly touch (John 13:10). (*Life-study of Exodus,* pp. 1674-1676)

Further Reading: Life-study of Ephesians, msgs. 56, 58

Enlightenment and inspiration: _____

_____

_____

_____

Morning Nourishment

Eph. And receive the helmet of salvation and the sword of
6:17-18 the Spirit, which *Spirit* is the word of God, by means
of all prayer and petition, praying at every time in
spirit and watching unto this in all perseverance and
petition concerning all the saints.
2 Cor. And the Lord is the Spirit; and where the Spirit of the
3:17 Lord is, there is freedom.
Rev. And He is clothed with a garment dipped in blood;
19:13 and His name is called the Word of God.

In Ephesians 6:17 Paul...speaks of "the sword of the Spirit,
which Spirit is the word of God." Among the six items of God's
armor, this is the only one for attacking the enemy. With the
sword we cut the enemy to pieces. However, we do not take up
the sword first. Rather, we must firstly put on the girdle, the
breastplate, and the shoes, and then take up the shield of faith
and the helmet of salvation. Then, when we are entirely protected
and have salvation as our portion, we may receive the sword of
the Spirit. (*Life-study of Ephesians*, p. 547)

Today's Reading

In Ephesians 6:17 the antecedent of the word *which* is *Spirit*,
not *sword*. This indicates that the Spirit is the word of God, both
of which are Christ (2 Cor. 3:17; Rev. 19:13). If I were writing this
verse, I would say, "the sword of the word of God." But Paul speaks
of "the sword of the Spirit, which Spirit is the word of God." Is the
sword here the sword of the Spirit or the sword of the word? Most
readers consider that Paul was saying that the sword is the word
and that the Spirit wields the sword. I understood the verse this
way for years. I thought that it was the Spirit, not I, who used the
sword. In other words, according to this understanding, the sword
is the word, and the One who uses the sword to slay the enemy is
the Spirit. From my youth I was taught that the Spirit helps us to
use the word of God as the sword. But this is not the meaning
here. The correct meaning is that the Spirit is the sword itself, not
the one who uses the sword. The word of God is also a sword. The

sword is the Spirit, and the Spirit is the word. Here we have three that are one: the sword, the Spirit, and the word.

My main burden...is on this matter. The Word is the Bible. But if this Word is only printed letters, it is neither the Spirit nor the sword. The Greek for *word* in verse 17 is *rhema*, the instant word spoken at the moment by the Spirit in any situation. When the *logos*, the constant word in the Bible, becomes the instant *rhema*, this *rhema* will be the Spirit. This *rhema*, which becomes the Spirit, is the sword that cuts the enemy to pieces. For example, we may read a particular verse again and again, only to have it remain the *logos*, a word in letters. Such a word cannot kill anything. But one day this verse becomes the *rhema* to us, the present, instant, living speaking. At that time this *rhema* becomes the Spirit. For this reason, in John 6:63 the Lord Jesus said, "The words which I have spoken to you are spirit and are life." Here the Greek text also uses *rhema*. The instant, present word is the Spirit. This kind of word is the sword. Therefore, the sword, the Spirit, and the word are three that are one. Furthermore, we, not the Spirit, are the ones to use this sword to kill the enemy.

In our Christian experience, the word and the Spirit must always be one. It is an utter falsehood to say that we take the Spirit without taking the word. Without taking the word, we cannot have the Spirit. In my experience, I receive the Spirit mostly through the word. As I contact the Word in a living way, it becomes the Spirit to me. However, some take the Bible without the Spirit. This also is wrong. Those who wish to grow flowers need both the seeds and the life contained in the seeds. It is impossible to separate the life within the seeds from the seeds themselves. In order to have the life, we must take the seeds. The relationship between the Word and the Spirit is like that between the seeds and the life. We must have both. The Lord Jesus is both the Spirit and the Word. He is not the Spirit without being the Word, nor the Word without being the Spirit. (*Life-study of Ephesians,* pp. 547-548)

Further Reading: Life-study of Ephesians, msg. 65

Enlightenment and inspiration: _____

_____

_____

_____

Morning Nourishment

John It is the Spirit who gives life; the flesh profits nothing;
6:63 the words which I have spoken to you are spirit and
are life.
1 Cor. So also it is written, "The first man, Adam, became a
15:45 living soul"; the last Adam *became* a life-giving Spirit.

Because He is both the Word and the Spirit, He created us with a mind to understand and a spirit to receive. When we come to the Bible, we should exercise both our mind and our spirit. We exercise our mind by reading and our spirit by praying. Since we need both to read and to pray, we should pray-read the Word....Through pray-reading my spirit becomes strong and ready to devour the enemy. I not only exercise my spirit, but I also exercise my mind to consider the Word....I also pray...[over whatever I consider]. The more my spirit is strengthened by pray-reading the Word, the more eager I am to use the sword of the Spirit to slay the enemy. In my speaking I have a sword with which to cut the enemy to pieces.

With the whole armor of God [in Ephesians 6] we have truth, righteousness, peace, faith, and salvation. Finally, we have the *rhema*, the Spirit, the sword. This is our offensive weapon to use in attacking the enemy. When we have the whole armor of God, including the sword, we are not only protected, but also prepared to wrestle against the enemy. By having truth, righteousness, peace, faith, and salvation we are equipped, qualified, strengthened, and empowered to use the sword in spiritual warfare. Then the enemy is subject to the cutting of our sword, and he is slaughtered by us. (*Life-study of Ephesians*, pp. 548-549)

Today's Reading

As we engage in spiritual warfare against the enemy, we do not use gimmicks, skills, or politics. Our only weapon is the Spirit-word, which is the sword. We do not employ cunning craftiness— we wield the sword of the Spirit. Our loins are girded with truth, and our conscience is covered by Christ as our righteousness. Then we have peace as our firm foundation. We can boast to the whole universe that we have no problems with God or man, for we are standing on the peace accomplished by Christ on the cross. Furthermore, we are protected by the shield of faith and guarded by the helmet of salvation. Therefore, when we pray-read the Word, every word becomes the *rhema,* the sword that cuts the enemy. In this way the victory is ours. We not only subdue the enemy and defeat him but slay him and even cut him into pieces. This is what it means to fight the spiritual warfare with the whole armor of God. The church must be such an equipped, fighting, and victorious church to slay God's enemy.

Pray-reading is a practical way to kill the negative elements within us. The more we take the word of God by means of all prayer in spirit, the more the negative things within us will be put to death. Thus, pray-reading is not only feasting; it is also a way of fighting. As we pray-read the word, the battle is raging as the negative elements in our being are slain. Eventually, the self, the worst foe of all, will be put to death. When the negative things in us are killed through pray-reading, the Lord is victorious. Because He is victorious, we are victorious also.

My concern...is not to present Ephesians 6 in a mere objective way. Instead, it is to help you experience Christ subjectively as all the aspects of the armor, especially as the sword of the Spirit. We have pointed out again and again that pray-reading is the way to kill the adversary within us. Every day and in every kind of situation, you should pray-read. Whenever you are troubled by something negative within you, take the word of God by means of prayer in spirit. As you do this, the negative element will be killed.

As we consider all these messages on the book of Ephesians, we need to thank the Lord that we are in His recovery. What a blessing it is to be in the Lord's recovery! Day by day, we enjoy inner satisfaction as we go forward under His blessing. The Lord will be victorious, He will gain all the ground within us, and He will prepare the way for His coming back. (*Life-study of Ephesians,* pp. 549-550, 821-822)

Further Reading: Life-study of Ephesians, msg. 97

Enlightenment and inspiration: _____

_____

_____

_____

Hymns, #1135

1   Oh, sanctify us, Lord; now add Thyself to us,
In our experience, Thy Person spread in us,
That in reality the church be glorious,
O Lord, do add Thyself, we pray.

Oh, sanctify us, Lord, today;
Lord Jesus, You're the only way.
We take Your Person, Lord;
Oh, spread Yourself abroad.
Oh, sanctify us, Lord, today.

2   Oh, purify us, Lord, by speaking in our heart;
Thy living, spoken word this washing will impart.
Increase Thy speaking, Lord, and cleanse our every part.
Oh, purify us, Lord, we pray.

Oh, purify us, Lord, today;
Wash all our natural life away.
Speak now Thy words in us,
And make us glorious.
O Lord, do speak in us today.

3   O Lord, do nourish us; You are the food we need;
As we are eating You, we'll be transformed indeed;
We're fully satisfied as on Yourself we feed,
So nourish us, O Lord, we pray.

O Lord, do nourish us today
As all our self You wash away.
Not only purify,
But fill and satisfy;
O Lord, do nourish us today.

4   O Lord, do cherish us, as on Thyself we feed;
Warm us so tenderly and meet our every need.
Our hardness soften, Lord, till we are Yours indeed;
Oh, cherish us, dear Lord, we pray.

O Lord, do cherish us today,
Until our coldness flees away.
Oh, hold us close to Thee
And cherish tenderly;
O Lord, do cherish us today.

5   Lord, make us glorious, by all Your inner work,
    Not glory for ourselves, but glory for the church;
    That You may have Your Bride, thus ending
    all Your search.
    O Lord, do work on us, we pray.

    O Lord, do work on us today!
    To form the church Your glorious way.
    Oh, spread Yourself in us
    Till we are glorious;
    Oh, make us glorious, Lord, today.

Composition for prophecy with main point and sub-points: _____

_____

_____

_____

_____

_____

_____

_____

_____

_____

_____

_____

_____

_____

_____

_____

_____

_____

_____

_____

_____

_____

_____

_____

_____

_____

Letting the Word of Christ
Dwell in Us Richly

Scripture Reading: Col. 3:16-17; Phil. 2:15-16

Day 1   I. **The word of Christ is the word spoken by Christ (Col. 3:16):**

   A. In His New Testament economy God speaks in the Son (Heb. 1:2; John 1:1, 14, 18):

   1. The Son speaks not only by Himself in the Gospels but also through His members—the apostles and prophets—in Acts, in the Epistles, and in Revelation (Matt. 17:5; Acts 4:20; 5:20; 6:7; Col. 1:25; Rev. 1:2, 9).

   2. All these speakings can be considered the word of Christ; thus, the word of Christ includes the entire New Testament (Col. 3:16).

   B. In Colossians the word is for revealing Christ in His preeminence, centrality, and universality (1:18; 2:9; 3:11):

   1. Colossians is focused on Christ as our Head and our life, and Paul's concern in Colossians is for the revelation of Christ unto full knowledge; for this, we need the word of Christ (1:9-10, 18; 2:19; 3:4, 10).

   2. The way for Christ to exercise His headship and to minister His riches to us is through His word; hence, the emphasis is on the word of Christ (Eph. 3:8; Col. 3:16).

Day 2   II. **The word of Christ is actually the person of Christ (v. 16; John 15:4, 7):**

   A. Paul almost personifies the word of Christ; he tells us to let this word dwell in us, as if it were a living person (Col. 3:16; cf. Eph. 3:17).

   B. First we have Christ as our life; then we have His living word personified as His person dwelling in us (Col. 3:4, 16).

   C. Since the word of Christ can dwell in us, it must be a living person; therefore, to let the word of Christ

dwell in us indicates that we allow a living person—
Christ Himself—to dwell in us (v. 16; 1:27).

D. If we would allow Christ to make His home in our
hearts, we must be filled with the word of Christ
(Eph. 3:17; John 14:23):

1. For the Lord's word to abide in us means that
the Lord Himself abides in us (15:4, 7).

2. If Christ is to abide in us in a practical way,
His words must abide in us; we cannot have
Christ in us experientially unless we have His
words in us also (Col. 1:27; 3:16; Eph. 3:17;
John 14:23; 15:4, 7).

Day 3   III. **We need to let the word of Christ dwell in us
richly (Col. 3:16):**

A. The Greek word rendered "dwell" literally means
to be in a house, to inhabit:

1. This indicates that we should allow the word
of Christ to dwell in us, to inhabit us, to make
home in us (v. 16).

2. The word of the Lord must have adequate
room within us so that it may operate and
minister the riches of Christ into our inner
being.

B. The word of Christ must dwell in us richly (v. 16):

1. The riches of Christ are in His word, and when
such a rich word inhabits us, it must inhabit
us richly (Eph. 3:8).

2. For the word of Christ to dwell in us richly
means that it inhabits us, indwells us, in a
rich way (Col. 3:16):

a. This can be illustrated by eating; when we
take nourishing food into us and assimilate it, it indwells us richly (John 6:57b).

b. In like manner, for the word of Christ to
dwell in us richly means that it inhabits us
in the way of nourishment and enrichment
(Matt. 4:4).

C. The word of Christ should have free course within
us; the word of Christ should be given the freedom

to operate within us, inhabiting us and making home in us (Col. 3:16).

Day 4   D. Instead of our culture, opinion, concept, thought, and view, we should have the word of Christ (Matt. 7:24; 16:23-24; 24:35):

1. We might not allow the word of Christ to dwell in us nor permit it to live, move, and act in us; as a result, what prevails in our being is our culture or philosophy, not the word of Christ (John 8:37, 47).

2. It is crucial that we let the word of Christ enter into us, dwell in us, and replace our culture, concept, opinion, and philosophy (Col. 1:5; 2:8; 3:16).

E. Negatively, we must set aside our cultural standards, and positively, we need to be filled with the word of Christ; this means that we must let the word of Christ fill our mind, emotion, and will and allow our whole being to be permeated and saturated with the word of Christ (vv. 10-11, 16).

Day 5 IV. **Allowing the word of Christ to dwell in us richly is related to doing all things in the name of the Lord Jesus (vv. 16-17):**

A. The word of Christ is actually the embodiment of Christ with all His riches; thus, to be saturated with the word is to be infused with and permeated by the riches of Christ (Eph. 3:8, 17).

B. As the word of Christ makes home in us, the Lord makes us one with Him, and spontaneously we can do things in the name of the Lord (Col. 3:16-17):

1. If we exercise our whole being to take in the word, eventually we will be filled, occupied, and saturated with the living word.

2. Because the word is the embodiment of the Spirit and because the Spirit is the reality of Christ, we will automatically be filled with Christ and do all things in the name of the Lord Jesus (John 6:63; 14:16-18; Col. 3:17).

Day 6   V. **If we let the word of Christ dwell in us richly,**

we will shine as luminaries in the world, holding forth the word of life (Phil. 2:15-16):

A. When we are filled with the word of life, we manifest Christ and magnify Him; this is the way to live Christ, who Himself is the word of life with which we shine (1:20-21a; 2:15-16).

B. The more we allow the word of Christ to dwell in us richly, the greater will be the accumulation of the word within us; then spontaneously we will shine with the word of life that we have taken into us (Col. 3:16; Phil. 2:15-16):

   1. This shining will then be our holding forth, our presenting of, the word of life to others (v. 16; Matt. 5:14-16).

   2. This is the proper preaching of the gospel and proclamation of the truth (Col. 1:5-6, 23; John 1:1, 14; 8:12, 32; 18:37).

Morning Nourishment

Col. And He is the Head of the Body, the church; He is the
1:18 beginning, the Firstborn from the dead, that He Him-
      self might have the first place in all things.
3:16 Let the word of Christ dwell in you richly in all wis-
      dom, teaching and admonishing one another with
      psalms *and* hymns *and* spiritual songs, singing with
      grace in your hearts to God.

We not only need to be filled in spirit by the processed Triune
God; we also need to let the word of Christ dwell in us richly. In
Colossians 3:16 Paul says, "Let the word of Christ dwell in you
richly." The word of Christ is the word spoken by Christ. In His
New Testament economy, God speaks in the Son, and the Son
speaks not only in the Gospels but also through His members,
the apostles and prophets, in Acts through Revelation. All these
books may be considered as His word. The word of Christ includes
the entire New Testament. We need to be filled with this word.
(*Truth Lessons—Level Three*, vol. 3, p. 116)

Today's Reading

Day by day when we come before the written Word, we should
feel that this living and personified word of Christ is waiting for
us and longing to dwell in us richly. Whenever we come before the
written Word, we should have the assurance deep within that we
are contacting the Lord Himself as the living Word. Therefore,
when we receive the word of Christ, that is, Christ Himself, we
should give the word the full freedom to make home in us. We
should pray, "Lord, I offer my whole being to You and to Your
word. I give You access to every part of my inner being. Lord,
make my inner being a home for Yourself and Your word."

Ephesians 5:18 charges us to be filled in spirit by the Triune God;
Colossians 3:16 tells us to let the word of Christ dwell in us richly.
Colossians is focused on Christ as our Head and life. The way for
Christ to exercise His headship and minister His riches into us is
through His word. Hence, the emphasis in Colossians is on the word
of Christ. Ephesians is concerned with the church as the Body of

Christ. The way for us to live a normal church life is to be filled in our spirit unto all the fullness of God. Hence, the Spirit is emphasized. In Ephesians both the Spirit and our spirit are emphasized again and again; the word is even considered to be the Spirit (6:17). However, in Colossians the Spirit is mentioned only once (1:8), and the human spirit is mentioned only once (2:5). In Ephesians the word is for washing away our natural life and fighting against the enemy (5:26; 6:17); in Colossians the word is for revealing Christ in His preeminence, centrality, and universality (1:25-27). This word, like the Spirit, is prepared to dwell in us, to occupy us, and to fill us, but we need to let the word dwell in us richly.

We enjoy the dispensing of the Divine Trinity by being filled in our spirit by the processed Triune God and letting the word of Christ dwell in us richly. Ephesians 5:18 says, "Be filled in spirit," and Colossians 3:16 says, "Let the word of Christ dwell in you richly." These two parallel portions of Scripture admonish us to be filled in our spirit by the Triune God and to let the word of Christ dwell in us richly. When we are filled in our spirit by the processed Triune God and let the word of Christ dwell in us richly, we enjoy the dispensing of the Divine Trinity. (*Truth Lessons—Level Three*, vol. 3, pp. 117, 114)

We need to allow the word of Christ to inhabit us. We should not be filled with Jewish tradition or Greek philosophy but with the word of Christ. We are containers of the word of Christ, not of philosophy or religion. We need to be emptied of all such things in order to be filled with the word of Christ. If we allow the peace of Christ to arbitrate in us and if we are filled with the word of Christ, we shall have the new man in a practical way. All the saints in all the churches throughout the Lord's recovery will be living Christ in the one new man....We care for Him as our life and as the constituent of the new man, not for our background, culture, opinion, and judgment. We want His peace to arbitrate in us and His word to fill us. (*Life-study of Colossians*, p. 300)

Further Reading: Truth Lessons—Level Three, vol. 3, lsn. 50; *The Healthy Word*, chs. 3, 8

Enlightenment and inspiration: _____

_____

_____

_____

Morning Nourishment

John Abide in Me and I in you. As the branch cannot bear
15:4 fruit of itself unless it abides in the vine, so neither
      can you unless you abide in Me.
7   If you abide in Me and My words abide in you, ask
      whatever you will, and it shall be done for you.

Colossians 3:16 says, "Let the word of Christ dwell in you
richly in all wisdom, teaching and admonishing one another with
psalms and hymns and spiritual songs, singing with grace in your
hearts to God." Here Paul says that the word of Christ should
dwell in us, inhabit us. This implies that the word of Christ is living. In order for something to dwell in us or to inhabit us, it must
be living.

Paul's expression in this verse indicates that the word of Christ
is very much like a living person. Paul almost personifies the
word of Christ; he tells us to let this word inhabit us, as if it were a
living person. The word of Christ is actually the living person of
Christ. (*Life-study of Philippians*, p. 353)

Today's Reading

First, we have Christ as our life, then we have His living Word
personified as His Person dwelling in us....The word of Christ
includes the entire New Testament. We need to be filled with this
word. This means that we should allow the word of Christ to
dwell in us, to inhabit us, to make home in us. The Greek word
rendered "dwell" literally means to be in a house, to inhabit. The
word of the Lord must have adequate room within us so that it
may operate and minister the riches of Christ into our inner
being. (*Elders' Training, Book 6: The Crucial Points of the Truth in
Paul's Epistles*, p. 96)

The word *dwell* in Colossians 3:16 indicates that the word of
Christ actually is a person—Christ Himself. Since the word can
dwell in us, make home in us, it must be a living person. Therefore, to let the word of Christ dwell in us indicates that we allow a
living person—Christ Himself—to dwell in us. (*Truth Lessons—
Level Three*, vol. 3, p. 116)

If we would allow Christ to occupy us and make His home in us, we must be filled with the word of Christ. In John 14:23 the Lord Jesus says, "If anyone loves Me, he will keep My word, and My Father will love him, and We will come to him and make an abode with him." Here we see the connection between the Lord's word and the Father and the Son coming to us and making an abode with us. It is difficult to say whether this abode is for the Father and the Son or for us. Actually, it is a mutual abode. On the one hand, the Lord makes us His abode; on the other hand, He is an abode to us. This is proved by the Lord's word in John 15:4 concerning abiding: "Abide in Me and I in you." This refers to the mutual abiding and to the mutual abode. No doubt, John 15 is the continuation of chapter fourteen. In chapter fourteen we have the mutual abode and in chapter fifteen, the mutual abiding. Because there is an abode both for the Lord and for us, we now can abide in Him and He can abide in us.

According to John 15:4 and 7, for the Lord's word to abide in us means that the Lord Himself abides in us. Verse 4 says, "Abide in Me and I in you." In verse 7 the Lord goes on to say, "If you abide in Me and My words abide in you...." These verses indicate that the Lord's words are equal to the Lord Himself. If Christ is to abide in us in a practical way, His words must abide in us. We cannot have Christ in us experientially unless we have His words in us also.

We praise the Lord that we have Christ, the Spirit, and the Word! Because Christ is God, He is real; because He is the Spirit, He is living; and because He is the Word, He is very practical. None of us can deny that, as those who believe in Christ, we have the Spirit and the Word. How wonderful that the Spirit and the Word are one!

When we are filled with the word of Christ, we are automatically filled with the riches of Christ and the fullness of the Godhead. (*Life-study of Philippians*, pp. 363-365)

Further Reading: Life-study of Philippians, msgs. 40-41; *Life-study of Colossians,* msg. 29*

Enlightenment and inspiration: _____

_____

_____

_____

Morning Nourishment

Eph. 3:8 To me, less than the least of all saints, was this grace given to announce to the Gentiles the unsearchable riches of Christ as the gospel.

John 6:57 As the living Father has sent Me and I live because of the Father, so he who eats Me, he also shall live because of Me.

We should allow the word of Christ to dwell in us, to inhabit us, to make home in us. The Greek word rendered "dwell" in Colossians 3:16 means to be in a house, to inhabit. The word of the Lord must have adequate room within us so that it may operate and minister the riches of Christ into our inner being. Furthermore, the word of Christ must dwell in us richly. The riches of Christ are in His word (Eph. 3:8). Such a word must inhabit us. We should not simply receive it and confine it to a small area of our being. On the contrary, it should be given a free course to operate within us. In this way the word will inhabit and make home in us. (*Truth Lessons—Level Three*, vol. 3, p. 116)

Today's Reading

Colossians 3:16 says, "Let the word of Christ dwell in you richly." You have to notice that in this verse Paul says, "Let the word of Christ dwell in you." This kind of tone indicates that the word of Christ is here waiting for you to let it come into you. It seems that a person is waiting here, waiting for you to let Him in. Years ago when I read this verse, I did not agree with this kind of tone. Why does Paul say, "Let the word of Christ dwell in you"? The indication here is that today the living word of Christ is waiting for you to let it in. This word is personified as a living person. You do not say, "Let the table dwell in your room." The table cannot dwell because it is lifeless. Anything that can dwell in your home must be a living person. A lifeless thing cannot dwell. Paul says, "Let the word of Christ dwell in you," and the New Testament tells us that Christ is the Word....Surely this is the organic Word, the living Word, the Word which exists as a living person. This Word is waiting to get into you. You have to open up yourself and let Him in. (*The Home Meetings—the Unique Way for the Increase and the Building Up of the Church*, p. 63) What does it mean to let the word of Christ dwell in us richly? Years ago I thought that this meant that we should memorize Bible verses and be able to recite them. According to my concept at the time, to let the word of Christ dwell in me richly was to memorize more and more verses. However, this is not the meaning of Paul's word in Colossians 3:16.

For the word of Christ to dwell in us richly means that it inhabits us, indwells us, in a rich way. This can be illustrated by eating. After we eat a meal, the food inhabits us in a rich way. The food contains many rich, nourishing elements. When we take this nourishing food into us and assimilate it, it indwells us richly. In like manner, for the word of Christ to dwell in us richly means that it inhabits us in the way of nourishment and enrichment. This is not a matter of memorizing verses, but a matter of having the Word containing the unsearchable riches of Christ dwell in us in such a way that it nourishes us and enriches us.

I have met some people who had memorized the whole book of Ephesians and even one who had memorized the Gospel of Matthew. But to memorize entire books of the New Testament does not mean that the word of Christ is dwelling in us richly. For example, we may take food into us, but our stomach may not digest it properly. Indigestion indicates that the food does not enter into us richly. The food may be rich in nourishment, but its entering into us is not rich if we suffer from indigestion after eating it. In such a case we do not have the ability to absorb the riches of the food. But if we have a proper metabolism and digest the food we eat, the elements of the food will enter into us richly. We need the word of Christ to dwell in us in this way. (*Life-study of Philippians*, p. 326)

Further Reading: Life-study of Philippians, msgs. 37-38; *Words of Training for the New Way*, vol. 2, ch. 22

Enlightenment and inspiration: _____

_____

_____

_____

Morning Nourishment

Col. Beware that no one carries you off as spoil through
2:8   his philosophy and empty deceit, according to the tra-
      dition of men, according to the elements of the world,
      and not according to Christ.

3:10-11 ...Put on the new man...where there cannot be Greek
      and Jew, circumcision and uncircumcision, barbarian,
      Scythian, slave, free man, but Christ is all and in all.

In Colossians the word is for revealing Christ (1:25-27) in His
preeminence, centrality, and universality. We have pointed out
that in Ephesians the emphasis is on the Spirit, whereas in Colossians the emphasis is on the word. Ephesians takes care of our
living, but Colossians takes care of the revelation of Christ. Paul's
concern in Colossians is for the revelation of Christ unto full
knowledge. For this, we need the word of Christ. (*Life-study of
Colossians*, p. 246)

Today's Reading

[Paul] emphasizes, on the one hand, the peace of Christ and,
on the other hand, the word of Christ. Some of us may think that
as long as our spirit is living, everything is all right. Perhaps you
have not realized the need for the peace of Christ to arbitrate
within you and for the word of Christ to make home in your heart.
If we let the peace of Christ work in us and the word of Christ
dwell in us, we shall be proper Christians. Instead of our prefer-
ence, we shall have Christ's arbitration. Instead of our opinion,
concept, thought, and estimation, we shall have Christ's word.

Certain saints love the Bible and read it daily. But in their living it is their concept, opinion, and philosophy that move within
them, not the word of Christ. They may study the Bible, but they
do not allow the word of Christ to dwell in them....As a result,
what prevails in their being is their philosophy, not the word of
Christ. Although they read the Bible, God's word remains outside
of them. It is crucial for us to let the word of Christ enter into us,
dwell in us, and replace our concepts, opinions, and philosophies.
We need to pray, "Lord Jesus, I am willing to let go of my concepts.

I want Your word to have ground in me. I am willing to forget my opinion and philosophy. I want Your word to be prevailing in me. I do not want my concepts to prevail any longer."

We cannot separate the word of Christ from His arbitration. The arbitrator settles a dispute by speaking a word. We need to bring our case to the arbitrator and listen to his word. This means that we need to allow the peace of Christ to arbitrate in our hearts and the word of Christ to dwell in us. Then we shall be filled with singing and giving of thanks.

According to Colossians 3:16, when the word of Christ dwells in us richly, we shall teach and admonish one another in psalms, hymns, and spiritual songs, singing with grace in our hearts to God. Teaching, admonishing, and singing are all related to the verb *dwell*. This indicates that the way to let the Lord's word dwell in us richly is by teaching, admonishing, and singing. We should teach and admonish not only in words but also in psalms, hymns, and spiritual songs.

Negatively, we must set aside our cultural standards, and positively, we need to be filled with the word of Christ. This means that we must allow the word of Christ to fill our mind, emotion, will, thought, and consideration. Every fiber of our being needs to be occupied by the word of Christ.

God's desire is that we live Christ moment by moment and leave no room for culture and philosophy. Our only practice should be the living person of Christ Himself. Second, we should lay aside our cultural standards. Our standard should not be any form of culture; it should be the indwelling peace of Christ. Third, we need to allow the word of Christ to fill our entire being. We need to let our whole being be permeated and saturated with the word of Christ. If we do these three things, we shall experience Christ spontaneously. Not only shall we have a lofty revelation of Christ, but we shall also experience Him in a practical way in our daily life. (*Life-study of Colossians,* pp. 246-247, 272)

Further Reading: Life-study of Colossians, msgs. 32-33, 36-37, 39, 41

Enlightenment and inspiration: _____

_____

_____

_____

Morning Nourishment

John It is the Spirit who gives life; the flesh profits
6:63   nothing; the words which I have spoken to you
       are spirit and are life.
Col.   Let the word of Christ dwell in you richly....And
3:16-17 whatever you do in word or in deed, *do* all things
       in the name of the Lord Jesus, giving thanks to
       God the Father through Him.

If a certain place is to become our home, we must have the
freedom to make all necessary arrangements. If we want to
keep a certain item, we may do so. But if we want to throw
something else away, we are free to do that as well. If we do not
have this kind of freedom, it is not possible for us to make that
place our home. In like manner, if the word of Christ is to
make its home in us, we must give it the full liberty, freedom,
and right. We need to pray, "Lord, I offer my whole being to
You and Your word. I give You access to every part of my inner
being. Lord, make my inner being a home for Yourself and
Your word." (*Life-study of Colossians,* p. 574)

Today's Reading

We all must confess that many times the Lord's word has
come to us, but we did not give it adequate room within us.
Instead, we limited the word of God and restricted it. Sometimes we do receive God's word, but we do not give it the freedom to make its home in us. Let me ask you, in your experience is the word of Christ first, or are you first? I do not believe
that anyone can say that first place is always given to God's
word. Sometimes we may give preeminence to the word of
Christ and allow it to be first. However, much more often we
ourselves are first. In a secret way we keep the first place for
the self. Outwardly we may act as if the first place is reserved
for the word of God. But secretly the first place is for us.

Many of us have learned from experience how difficult it is
for us to give first place to the word of God. For this, we need

the Lord's grace. We need to turn to the Lord and say, "Lord, I cannot do this, but, Lord, You can. Lord, I trust in You for this." (*Life-study of Colossians,* pp. 574-575)

In Colossians 3:17 Paul continues, "And whatever you do in word or in deed, do all things in the name of the Lord Jesus, giving thanks to God the Father through Him." This is the result of allowing the word of Christ to inhabit us. Doing all things in the name of the Lord Jesus is related to letting the word of Christ saturate us and permeate us. The word of Christ is actually the embodiment of Christ. Thus, when the word as the embodiment of Christ is mingled with our inner being, inwardly we are one with Christ. It is at such a time that we can spontaneously do things in the name of the Lord. Because the Lord has saturated us, permeated us, and mingled Himself with us, making us one with Him, we can do all things in His name.

To do things in the Lord's name is to do things in Him. The name denotes the person, and the Lord's person is the Spirit (2 Cor. 3:17a). Therefore, to do things in the name of the Lord is to act in the Spirit.

In the past, many of us did not exercise our whole being when we came to the Word. Often we used only our mind to study the Bible. We did not even exercise our emotion adequately to love the Word, or exercise our will strongly to receive the Word. But if we exercise our whole being to take in the Word, eventually we shall be filled, occupied, and saturated with the living Word. Because the Word is the embodiment of the Spirit and because the Spirit is the reality of Christ, we shall automatically be filled with Christ. Then whatever we do or say will be in the name of Christ. This is to live Christ. We live Christ automatically when we are saturated with the word of Christ through the Spirit. (*The Conclusion of the New Testament,* pp. 1689-1690)

Further Reading: Life-study of Colossians, msgs. 45, 49-50, 64

Enlightenment and inspiration: _____

_____

_____

_____

Morning Nourishment

Phil. That you may be blameless and guileless, children of
2:15-16 God without blemish in the midst of a crooked and
perverted generation, among whom you shine as
luminaries in the world, holding forth the word of
life, so that I may have a boast in the day of Christ
that I did not run in vain nor labor in vain.

If we are filled with the riches of the living Word day by day,
spontaneously we shall hold forth the word of life. We shall present the word of life to others and offer it to them. This is to magnify Christ and to live Christ. Christ Himself is the living Word,
the word of life. For this reason, when we are filled with the word
of life, we manifest Christ and magnify Him. This is the way to
live Christ. (*Life-study of Philippians,* p. 406)

Today's Reading

If we experience such a daily salvation, we will shine as luminaries, as lights, in the world, holding forth the word of life (Phil.
2:15-16). Our living holds forth, presents to people, the word of
life. On the one hand, we are preaching and teaching the word
of life; on the other hand, we are presenting the living word of life
by our living Christ. When we live Christ, we shine. We shine as
the lights of Christ, and that shining presents to others the word
of life. (*The Secret of Experiencing Christ,* p. 75)

Luminaries [Phil. 2:15]…reflect the light of the sun. The matter of shining as luminaries indicates our ability to function.
Praise the Lord that we are able to shine! We are not only children of God but are also luminaries with the heavenly function of
reflecting Christ as the real sun.

Every kind of life has its particular function. The function of
an apple tree is to bear apples, and our function as luminaries
possessing the divine life and nature is to shine. As sons of God
with the divine life, we have the function of shining. In our daily
living we should not merely behave ourselves according to a certain standard—we should shine.

As luminaries, we in ourselves do not possess any light. Our shining is simply the reflection of light which we receive from another source. Christ is the light, the real sun, and we reflect Him by holding forth the word of life. Thus, our shining is actually our reflection of Christ as the source of our light.

We shine by holding forth the word of life. According to Colossians 3:16, we should allow the word of Christ to dwell in us, to inhabit us, richly. Then we shall have the word of life with which to shine. In order to hold forth the word of life, we must first have the divine life within us. Because we are supplied with this life and energized by it, we can shine as luminaries by holding forth the word of life. The more we are nourished by feeding on the word of life, digesting and assimilating this word, the greater will be the accumulation of the word within us. Then spontaneously we shall shine with the very word of life we have taken into us. This shining will then be our holding forth, our presenting, the wonderful word of life to others. Those who have contact with us over a period of time will thus receive help from us. If we daily digest Christ as the word of life, accumulating the riches of the Word in a subjective, organic way, we shall have something living and organic to share with others. This is the proper gospel preaching and proclamation of the truth. As we have pointed out, this is the way to magnify Christ and live Him.

May we all pray-read the Word and sing the Word by exercising our spirit. May we be liberated from every kind of bondage in our dealing with the Word and the Spirit....Then our inner being will be filled with the riches of Christ. Spontaneously, unconsciously, and even unintentionally, we shall live a life that expresses Christ and holds forth the word of life. What the Lord needs in His recovery today is not a group of people who are religious, but a group of people who live Christ and who shine as luminaries by holding forth the word of life. (*Life-study of Philippians*, pp. 407-409)

Further Reading: Life-study of Philippians, msgs. 45-46; *The Secret of Experiencing Christ,* ch. 11*

Enlightenment and inspiration: _____

_____

_____

_____

Hymns, #1219

1   What a wonderful change in my living is wrought
    By saying Amen to God's Word.
    More of Christ into me at each instance is brought
    By saying Amen to His Word.

    Chorus:
    By saying Amen to His Word,
    By saying Amen to His Word,
    Thus the Lord takes my heart, and transforms
        every part,
    By saying Amen to His Word.

2   What I never could do God is doing in me,
    By saying Amen to His Word.
    And the change is so real all the brothers can see,
    By saying Amen to God's Word.

3   I have ceased from my wandering and going astray
    By saying Amen to God's Word.
    And my old inclinations are passing away
    By saying Amen to His Word.

4   Now the secret of faith in the Lord I can see—
    It's saying Amen to His Word.
    He is more real and precious than all things to me
    By saying Amen to His Word.

5   Now my love for the brothers abounds more and more
    By saying Amen to God's Word.
    And I'm being related as never before
    By saying Amen to His Word.

6   Now my hope in the Lord's soon return groweth bright
    By saying Amen to His Word.
    I am ready to see Him, my Lord, my delight,
    By saying Amen to His Word.

    Chorus:
    Lord Jesus, Amen to Your Word,
    Lord Jesus, Amen to Your Word.
    You are coming again—all my heart says Amen!
    Lord Jesus, Amen to Your Word!

Composition for prophecy with main point and sub-points: _____

_____

_____

_____

_____

_____

_____

_____

_____

_____

_____

_____

_____

_____

_____

_____

_____

_____

_____

_____

_____

_____

_____

_____

_____

_____

_____

_____

_____

_____

_____

_____

_____

_____

_____

_____

Living a Prophesying Life
to Speak the Word of God
in Ten Major Categories
for the Building Up of the Church

Scripture Reading: Psa. 45:1; Num. 11:29; 1 Cor. 14:3, 12, 31;
1 Pet. 4:11; 1 Cor. 12:8

*Day 1
&
Day 2* I. The speaking God, the Word of God, created us
in His image to be a speaking people (Gen. 1:26;
John 1:1; Heb. 1:1-2a; Acts 8:4; 1 Cor. 14:31).

 II. "My heart overflows with a good matter; / I
speak what I have composed concerning the
King. / My tongue is the pen of a ready writer"
(Psa. 45:1):

A. If we have an affectionate love for the Lord Jesus,
our tongue will be the pen of a ready writer, ready
to write our love and our praise.

B. Our heart should overflow to speak the full ministry of Christ in the stages of His incarnation, inclu-
sion, and intensification as the content of God's
eternal economy (John 1:14; 1 Cor. 15:45b; Rev. 1:4;
3:1; 4:5; 5:6).

III. Matthew 16:18 says, "I will build My church,"
and 1 Corinthians 14:4b says, "He who prophesies builds up the church":

A. To prophesy is to speak for the Lord and to speak
forth the Lord, that is, to dispense Christ into
people (vv. 3, 12, 31).

B. God's desire is for all of His people to be prophets
(Num. 11:29; 1 Cor. 14:31).

C. Christ first builds the church by dispensing Himself into us as the regenerating word of God
through those who prophesy by speaking Him
forth as the good news of the gospel (1 Pet. 1:23;
Rom. 10:14-17).

D. Christ continues to build the church by overflowing
from within us in the church meetings to speak
forth Christ into one another—to prophesy—for

the increase of Christ within us so that we may
grow with the growth of God for God's building
(John 7:37-39; Col. 2:19).

IV. **We must live a proper, normal Christian life—a
prophesying life—so that we may be the proper
speaking ones in the church meetings (1 Pet.
4:11):**
   A. We must love the Lord (John 21:15-17):
      1. The more we love the Lord, the more we are
         qualified, equipped, and perfected to speak for
         Him.
      2. Our love for the Lord is the factor, the ele-
         ment, and the very basic essence of our being
         powerful in speaking forth the Lord.
      3. If we love the Lord, we will surely be filled
         with Him, and we will surely have something
         of Him to pour out, to release the One who
         has filled us within.
   B. We must be revived by the Lord (Rev. 3:1-2, 15-17):
      1. Once we are revived, we will have a desire to
         go fishing for men and to go to the homes
         where the fish are (Matt. 4:19).
      2. To have a local church in the Lord's recovery
         that is living and prevailing with everyone
         speaking, we all need to be revived day by day
         (2 Cor. 4:16).
   C. We must live a victorious life, an overcoming life
      (Rev. 2:7, 11, 17, 26; 3:5, 12, 21).

Day 3   D. We must abide in the fellowship with the Lord
      daily and hourly (1 John 1:3, 6; 2 Cor. 13:14).
   E. We must be a praying person (Col. 4:2; Rom.
      10:12-13).
   F. We must enjoy the Lord every day early in the
      morning to have a new start of each day (Psa.
      119:147-148).
   G. We must learn to walk by and according to our
      spirit mingled with the Spirit (Gal. 5:16; Rom.
      8:4).
   H. We must live Christ for His magnification by the

bountiful supply of the Spirit of Jesus Christ (Phil. 1:19-21a; Gal. 2:20).

Day 4   I. We must speak Christ to all kinds of people daily in season and out of season (Acts 5:42; 8:4; 2 Tim. 4:2).

J. We must deal with our sins thoroughly (1 John 1:5, 7, 9; Acts 24:16).

K. We must be filled with the Spirit inwardly (13:52; Eph. 5:18).

L. We must be filled with the Spirit outwardly (Acts 4:31, 8; 13:9).

Day 5   M. We must accumulate the experiences of Christ (Phil. 3:8-10, 12-14).

N. We must keep a rich storage of the Lord's word (Col. 3:16; John 15:7; 1 John 2:14).

O. We must know some of the hymns on Christ, the Spirit, the church, life, etc., in our hymnal (1 Cor. 14:26; Eph. 5:19; Col. 3:16).

P. We must desperately endeavor to build up a habit of speaking in any meeting (1 Cor. 14:26, 4-5, 12, 31).

Q. We must always have something to speak in all the meetings as a freewill offering to God and to the audience (v. 26 and footnote 1).

Day 6 V. **We must be those who speak ten major categories of the word of God:**
A. The word of grace (Acts 20:32).
B. The word of truth (Eph. 1:13).
C. The word of the gospel (Acts 8:4).
D. The word of life (1 John 1:1; Phil. 2:16; Acts 5:20).
E. The healthy word (1 Tim. 6:3; 2 Tim. 1:13).
F. The edifying word (Eph. 4:29).
G. The good word (Heb. 6:5).
H. The word of righteousness (5:13).
I. The word of wisdom (1 Cor. 12:8).
J. The word of knowledge (v. 8).

VI. **The two most important items of the manifestation of the Spirit in the believers are the word of wisdom and the word of knowledge:**
A. According to the context of 1 Corinthians, the word

of wisdom is the word concerning Christ as the deeper things of God, predestined by God to be our portion (1:24, 30; 2:6-10).

B. The word of knowledge is the word that imparts a general knowledge of things concerning God and the Lord (8:1-7).

C. The word of wisdom is mainly out of our spirit through revelation, and the word of knowledge is mainly out of our understanding through teaching; the former is deeper than the latter.

D. However, both of these, not speaking in tongues nor any other miraculous gift, are listed as the first gifts and the topmost manifestation of the Spirit because both are the most profitable ministries, or services, for the edification of the saints and the building up of the church to carry out God's operation.

Morning Nourishment

Gen.   And God said, Let Us make man in Our image, ac-
1:26   cording to Our likeness; and let them have dominion
       ...over all the earth...

Heb.   God, having spoken of old in many portions and in
1:1-2 many ways to the fathers in the prophets, has at the
       last of these days spoken to us in the Son...

God is a speaking God. He created the universe and continues to do all things through His speaking. Therefore, everyone who has been saved and who has His life should learn to speak for Him and to speak His word.

The greatest mystery in the universe is God....This mystery is opened and revealed to us in His Word. Hebrews 1 tells us that our God is a speaking God (vv. 1-2). The speaking of the human race came from His creation. He is a speaking God, and He is also the Word. (*Speaking for God,* p. 41)

Today's Reading

God's desire...is that man speak for Him. This matter sounds easy to understand, but it contains a biblical mystery. God shows us clearly in the Bible that His purpose in creating man was that man might speak for Him. Genesis 1:26 says, "God said, Let Us make man in Our image, according to Our likeness." This was spoken during a council of the Divine Trinity to determine how to create man. The result was that God made man in His image.

Since God is a speaking God, when He created man in His image, He created man with the ability to speak, just like Himself.

Why is it that we human beings are able to speak? It is because we are God's representatives. He created us that we might represent Him. The most important requirement of a representative is that he must be able to speak. If today someone sends a representative to us, yet this representative...is not able to talk, then in the end no agreement can be reached since there is no possibility of having any discussion. This kind of representative is a useless representative. Today we can represent God because we can speak. ...We can speak because we are like God.

God created man with two outstanding features: one is that He created a spirit within man, and the other is that He created a speaking organ for man.

As God's representatives, we represent God; therefore, we must speak God's words. We have to speak for God and speak forth God; this God is the word.

After being regenerated in our spirit, we, the saved ones, are the children of God. As such, when we open our mouth, it ought to be God speaking; we speak whatever God speaks.

Since we were born of God, naturally we speak God's words. Since God's word is God Himself, when we speak God's word, we speak God.

The New Testament shows us that God wants us, the saved ones, to prophesy as prophets (1 Cor. 14:31). To prophesy is to speak the word of God instead of the word of demons or the word of man. The word of God is just God Himself; when we prophesy by speaking, we speak the word of God. Concerning this matter, Paul in the New Testament and Moses in the Old Testament (Num. 11:29) were in agreement. In 1 Corinthians 14:31 Paul said, "You can all prophesy one by one." Paul believed that every one of us can speak for God. The word *can* has two interpretations in Bible translation. The Chinese Union Version translates it into *may*. That everyone may prophesy means that everyone has the right, though not necessarily the ability, to prophesy. The Greek word has both meanings: *all may* and *all can*. Today as prophets, you and I, the saved ones, not only may but also can prophesy and speak for God.

It is very likely that Paul's concept came from Moses, because Paul...must have been familiar with what Moses had said in Numbers 11:29, "Oh that all Jehovah's people were prophets!"... Therefore, we see that this concept is consistent in both the Old and New Testaments—God wants His people to speak for Him. (*Speaking for God*, pp. 41-42, 43, 45, 47-48, 50)

Further Reading: Speaking for God, chs. 3-4

Enlightenment and inspiration: _____

_____

_____

_____

Morning Nourishment

Psa. My heart overflows with a good matter; I speak what
45:1 I have composed concerning the King. My tongue is
the pen of a ready writer.

Matt. And I also say to you that you are Peter, and upon this
16:18 rock I will build My church, and the gates of Hades
shall not prevail against it.

1 Cor. ...He who prophesies builds up the church.
14:4

[Psalm 45:1-8 is] the praise of Christ the King from four directions: His fairness (v. 2), His victory (vv. 3-5), His kingdom (vv. 6-7), and His virtues (v. 8). In this praise there are two balanced pairs: Christ's fairness and His victory, and Christ's kingdom and His virtues. Christ's fairness is balanced by His victory with its requirements (cf. Matt. 5:20; 25:14-30; John 15:2, 6), and His kingdom, the issue of His victory, is balanced by the sweetness of His virtues. (Psalm 45:1, footnote 1)

If we have an affectionate love for the Lord Jesus, our tongue will be the pen of a ready writer, ready to write our love and our praise. (footnote 2)

Today's Reading

For the God-ordained way, the biblical way, the new way, we all need, first of all, to love the Lord. In John 21 the Lord asked Peter if he loved Him. Peter told the Lord, "You know that I love You." Then the Lord answered, "Feed My lambs" and "Feed My sheep" (vv. 15, 17). To speak is not only to edify or to teach but also to feed the lambs and to feed the sheep. If we are going to feed the Lord's sheep, we have to speak. Without speaking, how could we feed any Christian? For us to feed the Lord's sheep, we must love Him. We should tell the Lord, "Lord, I love You, so I like to speak You forth to others." The more that we love Him, the more we are qualified, equipped, and even perfected to speak.

If we love the Lord, we surely will be filled with Him. Whatever fills us within will come out of us. The overflow comes from the infilling. When we love the Lord, He will fill us. From that day in 1925 when I gave my life to the Lord, I loved to study the Bible and to talk to people about Jesus. Because I was filled with the Lord Jesus, I wanted to speak the Lord Jesus. If we are filled with the Lord Jesus, we surely will have something to pour out. If the sisters love the Lord, they will not be able to restrain themselves from speaking forth the Lord. When we love the Lord to the uttermost, we must speak. We must release the One who has filled us within.

As we are loving the Lord, we will be revived. According to the book of Revelation, both the church in Sardis and the church in Laodicea were backsliding churches (3:1-2, 15-17). The Lord Jesus said to Sardis, "You have a name that you are living, and you are dead." Whatever the church in Sardis had was not growing but dying. They needed to repent. They needed a revival. Laodicea had become lukewarm. Because the saints of Laodicea were neither hot nor cold but lukewarm, the Lord was about to vomit them out of His mouth. They needed to repent. They needed a revival. The churches in the Lord's recovery need a revival to be brought out of such a lukewarm and dying situation.

If we are going to set up a denomination, we do not need a revival. But to have a local church in the Lord's recovery that is living and prevailing with everyone speaking, we all need to be revived.

Then we need to live a victorious life to overcome sin, to overcome the world, to overcome ourselves, to overcome our flesh, and even to overcome our quarreling with our spouse. The wives and the husbands among us may not be so one. Many couples may not have prayed together for three years. This is the situation that really needs a revival that we may live a victorious life. In each of the seven epistles to the seven churches in Revelation 2 and 3, the closing word is that we have to overcome (2:7, 11, 17, 26; 3:5, 12, 20-21). We need an overcoming life. (*Speaking Christ for the Building Up of the Body of Christ,* pp. 33-35)

Further Reading: Life-study of Ephesians, msg. 84; *Prophesying in the Church Meetings for the Organic Building Up of the Church as the Body of Christ (Outlines),* outline 1, pp. 10-11

Enlightenment and inspiration: _____

_____

_____

_____

Morning Nourishment

1 John
1:6
If we say that we have fellowship with Him and yet walk in the darkness, we lie and are not practicing the truth.

Psa.
119:147-
148
I anticipated the dawn and cried out; I hoped in Your words. My eyes anticipated the night watches, that I might muse upon Your word.

We also must abide in the fellowship with the Lord daily and hourly (1 John 1:6; 2 Cor. 13:14)....If I were not such a person, it would be hard for me to speak in the Lord's ministry. My speaking depends upon my continual and present fellowship with the Lord. Why can we not speak in the meetings? Maybe we have been absent from the Lord's fellowship for three days because we had a quarrel with our spouse....If we are going to speak for the Lord, we have to recover our fellowship with Him by confessing our sin and by making an apology to our spouse. We must remain, abide, in the constant and continual fellowship with the Lord. This is a strong demand.

We must also be praying persons. We should pray unceasingly all the day long. This means that we have to call on His name. We need to call, "O Lord." Do not think that such a short calling means nothing. It means a lot. While we are working in an office, teaching a class, or doing any task, we can call, "O Lord Jesus." Such a short calling means a lot to our Christian life. By calling on the name of the Lord, we can pray unceasingly. For us to be the speaking ones in our meetings we must be praying persons. (*Speaking Christ for the Building Up of the Body of Christ*, pp. 35-36)

Today's Reading

We also must enjoy the Lord in the Word every day early in the morning to have a new start of each day (Psa. 119:147-148). According to God's principle in His creation, He ordained to have a new year, a new month or a new moon, and a new day. Within every year we can have three hundred sixty-five new starts. If we failed for three hundred sixty-four days, we still have one more opportunity to have a successful day. We may have failed today, but thank the Lord tomorrow is still here waiting for us....There is a new chance for us to have a new start and be renewed.

We also must learn to walk by and according to our spirit mingled with the Spirit (Gal. 5:16; Rom. 8:4). Praise the Lord that we have a spirit and that our spirit is mingled with the divine Spirit! What a provision! Our God has created us with a spirit and has even regenerated our spirit. Immediately after regenerating us, He stays with us as the Spirit to be one with us and even to mingle Himself with us as one spirit (1 Cor. 6:17). Now we have such a mingled spirit. After having a good start in the morning, we should continue to walk, to live, to do everything by this mingled spirit and with this mingled spirit all day long. We must learn to practice this.

We must live Christ for His magnification by the bountiful supply of the Spirit of Jesus Christ, and this bountiful supply is right within us (Phil. 1:19-21; Gal. 2:20)....First, we have His Word in our hand. Second, we have the Holy Spirit, who is the bountiful Spirit of the Lord Jesus Christ, living in us, in our spirit, which has been regenerated and strengthened. We have such a provision, and we can live Christ by this divine provision. If we are such persons, we will surely have something to speak when we come to the meeting.

The Lord desires to recover a meeting with all the members speaking to function. But this depends upon our Christian walk. We must love the Lord, we must be revived, and we must live a victorious life. We must abide in the fellowship with the Lord daily and hourly, and we must be praying persons. We must enjoy the Lord in the Word early in the morning to have a new start of each day. We must walk and have our being by and according to the mingled spirit, and we must live Christ. If we are such persons day after day and throughout each day, we will be ready to speak in the meetings. Something of Christ will always be bubbling out of us. The Spirit will become a flow out from our innermost being to flow out all the riches of Christ by the Spirit (John 7:37-39). (*Speaking Christ for the Building Up of the Body of Christ*, pp. 36-39)

Further Reading: Speaking Christ for the Building Up of the Body of Christ, ch. 3

Enlightenment and inspiration: _____

_____

_____

_____

Morning Nourishment

2 Tim.   Proclaim the word; be ready in season *and* out of sea-
4:2   son; convict, rebuke, exhort with all long-suffering
         and teaching.

Acts   Because of this I also exercise myself to always have a
24:16   conscience without offense toward God and men.

In order to enrich and enliven our meetings, we must learn how to speak the word of the Lord in the Scriptures. We must learn to speak and not just read the word. We must also learn to have a corporate speaking of the word in our meetings....Everyone in the meeting should exercise his spirit and pay much attention to speaking and listening. When one speaks, the others should listen. When we have the speaking that utters and releases the holy word, the riches of God's word will be prevailing to touch all the attendants. We must practice this.

In order to be speaking ones in our meetings, we should be people with a proper character. Without a proper living, our speaking will have no backing. Our daily living, our character, what we are, is the real backing of our speaking....[We need to see a number of] points concerning the kind of persons we need to be so that we can be the proper speaking ones. (*Speaking Christ for the Building Up of the Body of Christ*, p. 41)

Today's Reading

We need to be those who speak Christ to all kinds of people daily in season and out of season (Acts 5:42; 8:4; 2 Tim. 4:2). We should speak Christ to people from every tribe, tongue, people, and nation (Rev. 5:9). In Mark 16:15 the Lord Jesus charged us to preach the gospel to all the creation. This indicates that we should pick up the burden for the preaching of the gospel to such an extent that we would speak to whatever is around us. We should speak to the mountains, the trees, the rivers, the animals, and the entire creation. If we practice this, we will become exercised in speaking. This will strengthen us to speak with power.

We also must be ones who deal with our sins thoroughly (1 John 1:9). We must be sin-dealing people. We should not tolerate sin in any way....We pick up the germs of sins, of trespasses, throughout the day, so we have to learn to wash ourselves by confessing all of our faults, shortcomings, wrongdoings, and trespasses.

We must have such a clearance within us if we are going to speak in the meetings or even if we are going to speak the gospel to anyone. Otherwise, our speaking will not be adequate or prevailing. When we do not have a clearance within our conscience in our fellowship with the Lord, our speaking will be reluctant. We will not have the full boldness because our conscience has been polluted....Paul said, "I...exercise myself to always have a conscience without offense toward God and men" (Acts 24:16). We must keep our conscience from all kinds of offenses....A conscience without offense is a conscience of clearance. When we have such a conscience, we can speak not only to the Lord but also to the unbelieving sinners with boldness....Regardless of whom we speak to, as long as we are speaking the word of God, Christ, or the gospel, we need a cleared conscience. In order for us to learn to speak in the meetings, we must get ourselves cleared up and preserved in a clear condition. We must deal with our sins thoroughly.

Furthermore, we need to be filled with the Spirit inwardly (Acts 13:52; Eph. 5:18). We need the essential filling of the essential aspect of the Spirit. The Spirit in its essential aspect, the Spirit of essence, the Spirit of life, is for our being, our life, our living, our existence. We have to be filled essentially in our inward being with such a Spirit....To be filled with the Spirit outwardly is the economical aspect of the Spirit (Acts 4:31, 8; 13:9). It is the economical filling of the economical Spirit. We must have the Spirit of power economically for our work, for our doing, for our moving. We all need to be filled with the Spirit in His two aspects—we need to be filled inwardly so that we are full of life and filled outwardly so that we are full of power and authority. (*Speaking Christ for the Building Up of the Body of Christ*, pp. 41-45)

Further Reading: Speaking Christ for the Building Up of the Body of Christ, ch. 4

Enlightenment and inspiration: _____

_____

_____

_____

Morning Nourishment

Col. Let the word of Christ dwell in you richly in all wis-
3:16 dom, teaching and admonishing one another with
psalms *and* hymns *and* spiritual songs, singing
with grace in your hearts to God.

1 Cor. What then, brothers? Whenever you come together,
14:26 each one has a psalm, has a teaching, has a revelation, has a tongue, has an interpretation. Let all
things be done for building up.

In order to be the speaking ones in our meetings, we must also accumulate the experiences of Christ. From Philippians 3:8-10 and 12-14, we can see that Paul was accumulating the experiences of Christ day after day....Before he was saved, Paul persecuted Christ. After being saved, Paul continued to persecute Christ in a positive sense. He would not let the Lord go; he pursued Christ to the uttermost. Because he sought after Christ in such a way, he accumulated the experiences of Christ continually....This is why Paul had so much to say about Christ.

We also must keep a rich storage of the Lord's word (Col. 3:16; John 15:7; 1 John 2:14). If we would just practice to pray-read two to four verses from the Word every morning, and we do this week after week and month after month, we will gain a rich storage of the living word. The word will not just be in our memory, but it will be something stored within us....The riches of Christ are embodied in the holy Word. This is what makes the Bible different from all the other books....We have the same experience whenever we read the publications of the ministry that expound the Bible in the way of life. (*Speaking Christ for the Building Up of the Body of Christ*, pp. 47-48)

Today's Reading

The speaking ones in our meetings must know some of the hymns on Christ, the Spirit, the church, life, etc. in our hymnal (1 Cor. 14:26; Eph. 5:19; Col. 3:16). If we want to know the hymnal, we must spend some time to get into the table of contents of our hymnal. The hymns are divided into thirty major categories arranged in a proper sequence according to the truth. Each major category has a number of subcategories....We have to learn to use the hymns firstly for speaking. Singing the hymns is not as important as speaking them. We have discovered in the Word and in our experience that speaking a hymn is much more important and profitable than singing it. *Hymns,* #501—"O glorious Christ, Savior mine"—and hymn #539—"O Lord, Thou art the Spirit!"—are... excellent hymns that we should know and learn to speak. We must endeavor to learn a number of the crucial hymns in our hymnal.

We all have to desperately endeavor to build up a habit of speaking in any meeting (1 Cor. 14:26, 4-5, 12, 31)....This habit has to be built up universally in the Lord's recovery. We do not have such a habit due to the background of Christianity, and our function has been killed because of this background. Many Chinese people do not speak English well because they did not have the habit of speaking English when they grew up, and they still do not have this habit. I did not pick up the habit of speaking English until I began to minister the word in the United States in 1962. It was hard for me to acquire this habit, but for my grandchildren it was easy because they grew up in an English-speaking environment. If we learn to build up a habit of speaking in any meeting, our children, the new ones, will spontaneously become speaking ones. The new ones will follow the trend and the atmosphere in the meeting. They will pick up the habit of speaking easily. We must endeavor to do this because it is not just for ourselves but for the benefit of the Lord's recovery.

We should always have something to speak in all the meetings as a freewill offering to God and to the audience (1 Cor. 14:26 and footnote 1). In all our meetings we should not speak merely out of being forced or compelled to speak. Our speaking should be an offering of our free will to God for His glory and satisfaction and to the attendants for their enlightening, nourishing, and building up. (*Speaking Christ for the Building Up of the Body of Christ,* pp. 49-52)

Further Reading: Prophesying in the Church Meetings for the Organic Building Up of the Church as the Body of Christ (Outlines), outline 8, pp. 51-54

Enlightenment and inspiration: _____

_____

_____

_____

Morning Nourishment

John **And the Word became flesh and tabernacled among**
1:14 **us...full of grace and reality.**
Acts **...They did not cease teaching and announcing the**
5:42 **gospel of Jesus *as* the Christ.**
1 Cor. **For to one through the Spirit a word of wisdom is**
12:8 **given, and to another a word of knowledge, accord-**
ing to the same Spirit.

There are ten major categories of the word of God....First, the word of grace and the word of truth are a pair. Second, the word of the gospel and the word of life are another pair. Third, the healthy word and the building-up word are also a pair. The good word and the word of righteousness are the fourth pair, and the word of knowledge and the word of wisdom are the final pair. Altogether these constitute ten categories of the word of God. To speak the word of God to people is to speak these ten major categories of the word. (*Everyone Speaking the Word of God,* pp. 32-33)

Today's Reading

The Lord Jesus is the Word of God [John 1:1, 14]....[Footnote 5 on verse 14 and footnote 1 on verse 17] explain clearly that grace is God coming to be enjoyed by us. The Lord Jesus is God. When He became flesh, He brought God to man, and the God whom He brought is grace. When God is enjoyed by us, He is grace. At the same time, when this God is realized by us, He is reality, which is the proper meaning of the word *truth*. The word *truth* in Greek means "reality." God is grace and God is reality. When God is enjoyed by us, He is grace, and when God is realized by us, He is reality.

The third category is the word of the gospel. The gospel is the Lord Jesus Himself [Acts 5:42]....Romans 1:1 and 3 speak of "the gospel...concerning His Son, Jesus Christ our Lord." Thus the gospel is the Son of God. Therefore, to speak the word of the gospel is to speak the Lord Jesus. The more we speak the Lord Jesus, the more we speak the word of the gospel....One of the major points of the gospel is life....The Word of life [in 1 John 1:1] denotes the Lord Jesus.

Now we come to the healthy word. Some words are not healthy, but all healthy words contain life, and health pertains to life....If you desire to speak healthy words, you must have life. Healthy words surely are words with life....Furthermore, we must speak words that build up people. Ephesians 4:29 says, "Let no corrupt word proceed out of your mouth, but only that which is good for building up, according to the need, that it may give grace to those who hear." Grace is God Himself. Words which contain God are good words, and they will build up people.

The book of Hebrews speaks of...the good word and the word of righteousness (6:5; 5:13)....Paul advised the Hebrew believers not to remain in the good word but to go forward to the word of righteousness. He likened the good word to milk and the word of righteousness to solid food.

You can all differentiate between the word of knowledge and the word of wisdom....[1 Cor. 12:8]. The deeper and higher word is the word of wisdom; the shallower and lower word is the word of knowledge. The words written by Paul in 1 Corinthians chapter one are somewhat general; thus they are the word of knowledge. ...However, in chapter two Paul said, "But we do speak wisdom... God's wisdom in a mystery, the wisdom which has been hidden, which God predestined before the ages for our glory" (vv. 6-7). This is deep. This wisdom is the deep and mysterious things of Christ, which are also the deep and mysterious things of God (v. 10). In chapter three Paul speaks on the deep and mysterious things.... These words seem shallow and easy to understand, but their meaning is very deep. These are words of wisdom. However, to speak concerning the crucifixion of Jesus...and concerning the fact that we all are sinners—these are words of knowledge. But whenever life is mentioned, that is something deep and mysterious....In 6:17 Paul said that we the believers have become one spirit with the Lord; this is very difficult to speak about, and this is not shallow or easy to understand. We need to labor properly upon words such as these. (*Everyone Speaking the Word of God*, pp. 33-37)

Further Reading: Everyone Speaking the Word of God, chs. 3-4

Enlightenment and inspiration: _____

_____

_____

_____

Hymns, #1294

1 Come let us speak till the kingdom of the
   Lord comes down.
   Yes, let us speak till the kingdom of the
   Lord comes down.
     Why hold your peace?
     The Word release.
   Let us speak until the kingdom of the Lord
   comes down.

2 Oh, loose the Word! It shall not return
   unto Him void.
   Yes, loose the Word! It shall not return
   unto Him void.
     Let's sow the seed,
     This is our need;
   Loose the Word, and it shall not return
   unto Him void!

3 It's gospel time! Let us spread the gospel
   all around.
   Yes, gospel time! We will never fear the
   people's frown!
     God's done His work;
     Let us not shirk;
   We're but pilgrims here, and we'll not fear
   the people's frown!

4 If we will speak, Christ will witness in the
   hearts of men.
   If we will speak, Christ will witness in the
   hearts of men.
     Tell every man,
     Win all we can.
   Through our speaking, Christ is speaking
   in the hearts of men!

5 The harvest's ripe! We are preaching the
   full gospel now!
   The fields are white! We are preaching the
   full gospel now!
     For this men search—
     Christ and the church!
   Let us reap the harvest, preaching the
   full gospel now!

Composition for prophecy with main point and sub-points: _____

_____

_____

_____

_____

_____

_____

_____

_____

_____

_____

_____

_____

_____

_____

_____

_____

_____

_____

_____

_____

_____

_____

_____

_____

_____

_____

_____

_____

_____

_____

_____

_____

**The Word of God Growing,
Multiplying, and Prevailing,
Being Experienced
in the Word of Righteousness,
and the Need for the Speaking
of God-constituted Persons**

Scripture Reading: Acts 6:7; 12:24; 19:20; 20:32; Heb. 5:13-14; Gen. 47:7; 49:28

*Day 1
&
Day 2*

I. **When all the members of the Body of Christ speak for God, the word of God grows, multiplies, and prevails (Acts 6:7; 12:24; 19:20):**
   A. Following the death of Stephen, those who were scattered because of the persecution against the church "went throughout the land announcing the word" (8:4):
      1. What we need today is for all the saints to speak the word of God; if we all speak, the word of God will grow, multiply, and prevail (6:7; 12:24; 19:20).
      2. Eventually, our speaking the word of God will cause the Lord Jesus, the Word of God, to come and fight for His kingdom (Rev. 19:11, 13, 16).
   B. Satan wants to prevent the believers from speaking for God (Acts 5:28, 40).
   C. The word *grew* in Acts 6:7 refers to the growth in life:
      1. The word of God is a matter of life that grows as a seed sown into man's heart (Mark 4:14).
      2. God's word is the seed of life; because this seed is living, once it is planted, it grows, increases, and spreads (1 Pet. 1:23-25).
      3. The word of God is actually the Lord Himself because the word is the container of the Lord; thus, for the word of God to grow actually means that the Lord grows (Mark 4:26-29; Col. 2:19; Eph. 3:17; 4:13, 15-16).

D. In Acts the word of God not only grew but also multiplied (12:24):
   1. The word does not grow and multiply in itself but grows with the believers and multiplies with the churches (6:7; 9:31):
      a. When the believers grow, the word within them grows (Col. 3:16).
      b. When the churches multiply, the word multiplies within the churches.
   2. The fact that the word of God grew and multiplied indicates that the believers and the churches were filled with the word and were one with the word; this is a strong sign of the Lord's victory over the evil one (v. 16).
E. In order for the word of God to grow, multiply, and prevail, we need to enjoy the word of God's grace; we should receive the word of grace in such a way that we become God's word, that is, God's speaking (Acts 14:3; 20:32).
F. If the word of God is to grow, multiply, and prevail, we need to pray that God would open a door for the word, that the word of God would run and be glorified, and that we all would speak the word of God with boldness (Col. 4:3; 2 Thes. 3:1; Acts 4:29, 31).

Day 3 II. **We need to be experienced in the word of righteousness (Heb. 5:13-14):**
A. The word of righteousness is solid food; to eat the word of righteousness is a strong way to receive, experience, and enjoy Christ (vv. 13-14).
B. The word of righteousness speaks of the present Christ, who is now in the heavens as our Minister and our High Priest, ministering to us the heavenly life, grace, authority, and power and sustaining us to live a heavenly life on earth (4:14-15; 7:26; 8:2):
   1. In order to be brought on to maturity, we need to be experienced in the word of righteousness (6:1; 5:13-14).
   2. If we are exercised in the word of righteousness

concerning the heavenly ministry of Christ, we will reach maturity and receive a reward; otherwise, we will suffer dispensational punishment (4:11; 6:8; 10:35; 12:25, 28-29).

Day 4

C. The word of righteousness embodies the thought of God's justice and righteousness in His dispensational and governmental dealings with His people (5:13):

1. Righteousness is being right with persons, matters, and things according to God's righteous requirements (Matt. 5:20).
2. Righteousness is a matter of God's kingdom, for it is related to God's government, administration, and rule (6:33; Psa. 89:14; Isa. 32:1).

Day 5

3. Righteousness is a matter of being right with God in our being (1 Cor. 15:34):
   a. To be right with God in our being is to have an inner being that is transparent and crystal clear—an inner being in the mind and will of God (Col. 1:9; 3:1-2).
   b. To be righteous in this way is to become the righteousness of God in Christ (2 Cor. 5:21).

D. We need to be experienced in the word of righteousness so that we may have the words we need to speak for God, even being a herald of righteousness, as Noah was (Heb. 5:11-14; 2 Pet. 2:5).

Day 6

III. **In the church life today, there is the need for the speaking of God-constituted persons—those who have the maturity in life to prophesy with blessing, as Jacob did (Gen. 49:1-28; 2 Cor. 13:3; 1 Cor. 7:25, 40):**

A. The strongest sign of Jacob's maturity was his blessing others (Gen. 47:7, 10):

1. The fullness of life is blessing, which is the overflow of God as life into others (48:14-16; Heb. 7:7; John 7:38; 1 John 5:16).
2. Jacob's prophesying with blessing in Genesis 49 is a manifestation of maturity, for our speaking always reveals where we are and

how mature we are; the change in Jacob's speaking reveals his growth unto maturity (1 Cor. 3:1-4; Gen. 25:31; 27:19; 47:7).

3. Eventually, Jacob became a God-constituted person; because he had been infused, saturated, and thoroughly permeated with God, his word was God's word, and his speaking was God's speaking (49:1-28).

B. If we have been constituted with God, we will be able to prophesy with blessing, overflowing God as life into others (Heb. 6:1; Eph. 4:13).

C. When a God-constituted person ministers the word of God in spirit, apparently it is he who is speaking, but actually it is Christ, the Son of God, speaking; this minister of the word is nothing, but out of his lips comes something from the One who is everything (2 Cor. 11:10; 13:3; 1 Cor. 7:17-25, 40; Eph. 3:8).

D. What the churches need today is the speaking of such God-constituted persons (2 Cor. 13:3).

Morning Nourishment

Acts And the word of God grew, and the number of the
6:7   disciples in Jerusalem multiplied greatly; and a
      large number of the priests obeyed the faith.
12:24 But the word of God grew and multiplied.
19:20 Thus, the word of the Lord grew mightily and pre-
      vailed.

The word *grew* [in Acts 6:7] refers to growth in life. This indicates that the word of God is a matter of life that grows as a seed
sown into man's heart (Mark 4:14). (*Life-study of Acts*, p. 159)

In Acts we are told three times that the word grew and that
the word multiplied (Acts 6:7; 12:24; 19:20). A lifeless thing can
never grow but the word grows. Actually, the multiplication of
the disciples depends upon the growth of the word. However,
many who read Acts would mostly pay their attention to the
Spirit. No doubt, the Spirit is stressed in Acts. But those who
received the Spirit did not go out and preach the Spirit. Rather,
they preached the word. Many verses in Acts tell us that what
was preached and taught by the first group of believers was the
word. The scattered ones in Acts 8 went out to bring the good
news of the word (vv. 1, 4). People believed in the word, received
the word, and the word became so prevailing in that it grew
and multiplied. In Acts 12 is a very meaningful contrast. King
Herod was persecuting the church and especially Peter, but
eventually Herod died (v. 23). Right after his death Acts 12:24
says, "But the word of God grew and multiplied." The persecu-
tor died but the word grew. (*Elders' Training, Book 5: Fellowship concerning the Lord's Up-to-date Move*, pp. 37-38)

Today's Reading

The word of God is actually the Lord Himself because the
word is the container of the Lord. Therefore, for the word of God
to grow actually means that the Lord grew.

Acts 12:24 says that the word of God not only grew but also
multiplied. The word does not grow and multiply in itself.
Rather, the word grows with the believers and multiplies with

the church. When the believers grow, the word within them grows. When the churches multiply, the word multiplies within the churches. The fact that the word of God grew and multiplied indicates that in ancient times the believers and the churches were filled with the word and were one with the word. This is a strong sign of the Lord's victory in His battle against the evil one.

The growth and multiplication of the word in 12:24 was the result, the issue, of Peter's ministry....The last word concerning his ministry in Acts is that the word of God grew and multiplied. This is a glorious and victorious ending of Peter's ministry. (*Life-study of Acts*, pp. 294-295)

The book of Acts mentions three times that the word of God "grew" (6:7; 12:24; 19:20). The Bible reveals that God's word is the seed of life (1 Pet. 1:23-25). Because this seed is living, once it is planted it grows, increases, and spreads.

As for God's word, in Acts 6:4 Peter said, "But we will continue steadfastly in prayer and in the ministry of the word." This indicates that the word of God needs to be preached. On the one hand, if we do not properly read the word of God, we cannot preach it. On the other hand, if we do not preach the word of God, we cannot properly read it. We may illustrate this with teaching. On the one hand, a person cannot be a teacher unless he is first a student. On the other hand, those who are teachers know that regardless of how well they study from books, mere studying cannot be compared to teaching, because the need to teach forces them to read thoroughly. Therefore, in order to preach, one must read, and when one reads, he must preach. (*Rising Up to Preach the Gospel*, pp. 66-67)

Further Reading: Life-study of Acts, msgs. 19, 34; Elders' Training, Book 5: Fellowship concerning the Lord's Up-to-date Move, ch. 3; Rising Up to Preach the Gospel, ch. 4; Speaking for God, ch. 3; Three Crucial Matters for the Increase and Building Up of the Church: Begetting, Nourishing, and Teaching, ch. 16

Enlightenment and inspiration: _____

_____

_____

_____

Morning Nourishment

Col.
4:3

Praying at the same time for us also, that God would open to us a door for the word, to speak the mystery of Christ...

2 Thes.
3:1

Finally, brothers, pray concerning us, that the word of the Lord may run and be glorified, even as *it is* also with you.

Acts
4:31

And when they had *so* besought, the place in which they were gathered was shaken, and they were all filled with the Holy Spirit and began to speak the word of God with boldness.

The divine word is what we really need and we should be one with the word, full of the word, saturated with the word, and constituted with the word. Then when we minister, we minister the word by the Spirit. We do not minister the Spirit by the word, but we minister the word by the Spirit. In chapter four of Acts, while the disciples and the apostles were praying, they were filled with the Spirit and began to speak the word with boldness (Acts 4:31). They did not teach or preach the Spirit; the Spirit was only the power for them to preach the word. (*Elders' Training, Book 5: Fellowship concerning the Lord's Up-to-date Move*, p. 38)

Today's Reading

[Now] we come to the point of the word of God increasing, multiplying, and prevailing. First, we need to pray for the word of God, asking God to open a door for His word....Not only do the unbelievers need a door to be opened among them; even many Christians in the denominations, especially those in the Catholic Church, need God to open a door among them, because they themselves have closed the door. Because they lack enlightenment, they have fallen into darkness, thinking that they already know the truth but not actually understanding it. Today the Lord has opened His Word not for us only, but for all the Christians, even for the people of the whole world. We need to pray, "Lord, open the door for us." Paul asked the believers to pray "that God may open to us a door for the word, to speak the mystery of Christ" (Col. 4:3).

Second, Paul said, "Pray concerning us, that the word of the Lord may run and be glorified" (2 Thes. 3:1). Running is a matter of the way. Once the door is opened, there is still the need to have a way. Ordinarily, people walk on the way first and then go through the door. But according to the Bible, we first must go through the door, and then we can walk on the way (Matt. 7:14). As soon as the door is opened, the way is wide open to let the word of God run and be glorified.

Acts 12:24 says, "The word of God grew and multiplied." This growth and multiplication of the word took place in three stages in the book of Acts. The first stage was during the ministry of Peter. During this time Acts 6:7 says that "the word of God grew." The second stage was at the time when Peter's ministry was coming to an end. Although Peter was put into prison, God released him from that prison, and as a result "the word of God grew and multiplied" (Acts 12:24). The last stage was in Paul's ministry. While Paul was in Ephesus, he prevailed greatly in the struggle for the truth. Therefore, Acts 19:20 says, "So the word of the Lord grew mightily and was strong."

In Revelation 19 the Lord Jesus coming down out of heaven appears as a general fighting a battle. He is riding on a white horse, and His name is called "the Word of God" (Rev. 19:11, 13). The word of God that we speak today is the Lord Jesus. Eventually, as we continue to speak, our speaking will cause the Lord Jesus to come forth. When the Lord comes, He comes as a warrior, a general. On His garment and on His thigh the name "King of kings and Lord of lords" is written (Rev. 19:16). He is fighting for His kingdom. (*Everyone Speaking the Word of God*, pp. 57-58)

Further Reading: Everyone Speaking the Word of God, ch. 5; Life-study of Acts, msg. 55

Enlightenment and inspiration: _____

_____

_____

_____

Morning Nourishment

Heb. **For everyone who partakes of milk is inexperienced**
5:13—6:1 **in the word of righteousness, for he is an infant; but**
solid food is for the full-grown, who because of prac-
tice have their faculties exercised for discriminating
between both good and evil. Therefore leaving the
word of the beginning of Christ, let us be brought on
to maturity, not laying again a foundation of repent-
ance from dead works and of faith in God.

To eat the word of righteousness as the solid food (Heb. 5:13-14) is a strong way to receive, experience, and enjoy Christ. The word of righteousness is the solid food. Hebrews is divided into five sections, and each section ends with a warning concerning the coming kingdom (2:1-4; 3:7—4:13; 5:11—6:20; 10:19-39; 12:1-29). If we do not heed the warnings, we will suffer punishment and lose the kingdom in the millennium. Many in today's Christianity not only do not understand this word but even oppose it. Some...say that if Christ can punish His redeemed ones, then His redemption is not complete. It is true that Christ's redemption is complete, but Hebrews tells us that God chastises those whom He receives (12:6). God's chastisement is not against Christ's redemption. Moreover, there is no word in the New Testament that says that God chastises His people only in this age and not in the next. In nearly every book of the New Testament we are warned concerning the possibility of being chastened by God in the coming age. We must live a life of the highest righteousness. If we do, we will enter into the kingdom of the heavens and enjoy it as a reward (Matt. 5:20). Otherwise, according to the Lord's word in the Gospels, we will be cast into outer darkness, where there will be the weeping and the gnashing of teeth, as a kind of chastisement (25:30). (*The Central Line of the Divine Revelation*, pp. 216-217)

Today's Reading

Paul told the Hebrews that they had tasted of the heavenly gift, had become partakers of the Holy Spirit, and had tasted the good word of God and the powers of the coming age (Heb. 6:4-5). However, he also told them that he had deeper things to say to them that they were not able to understand (5:10-12). The word of righteousness...is solid food. It is difficult to take, but it is solid and it sustains long. (*The Central Line of the Divine Revelation*, p. 217)

The book of Hebrews conveys to us the word of righteousness. The word of righteousness tells us that this resurrected Christ has ascended to the heavens and is now serving as the Minister in the better tabernacle in the heavens. He is our great High Priest, the Mediator of the new covenant, carrying out His heavenly ministry and infusing us with the fullness of the heavenlies, with His ascension, resurrection, and life, making us heavenly persons on earth. This ministry will bring us to maturity. If we are willing to go on in this way, receiving the heavenly ministry of Christ, we will certainly reach maturity. When the Lord comes, He will give us the reward and we will enter into the kingdom. If we do not reach maturity, however, we need to realize that our God is a consuming fire and that we may be burned by His righteous judgment. This is the word of righteousness.

How do we become mature? We need to listen to the word of righteousness. The resurrection of Christ was not the end but the beginning of His heavenly ministry. He ascended to the heavens to be the better Minister to serve us in the better tabernacle in the heavens, supplying us with His heavenly life. He is the great High Priest in the heavens who intercedes for us. He is also the Mediator of the new covenant, who is executing all the bequests and blessings of the new covenant into us, causing us to grow and mature. When He comes back, we will either receive the reward and enter into the kingdom, or we will suffer punishment (not eternal perdition). This kind of word is not the good word but the word of righteousness. (*Everyone Speaking the Word of God*, pp. 43-44)

Further Reading: The Central Line of the Divine Revelation, msg. 18; *Everyone Speaking the Word of God*, ch. 4; *The Advance of the Lord's Recovery Today*, ch. 4; *Bearing Remaining Fruit*, vol. 1, chs. 5, 10

Enlightenment and inspiration: _____

_____

_____

_____

Morning Nourishment

Heb.   **For when because of the time you ought to be teachers,**
5:12-13   **you have need again for someone to teach you what**
the rudiments of the beginning of the oracles of God
are and have become those who have need of milk
and not of solid food. For everyone who partakes of
milk is inexperienced in the word of righteousness...

The first category of the word is the word of the beginning of Christ which is the good word of God [Heb. 6:1, 5], and in 5:13 is another category—the word of righteousness....The beginning of the oracles of God [in verse 12] equals the word of the beginning of Christ. Milk in 5:13 refers to the rudiments of the beginning of the oracles of God mentioned in verse 12, whereas the word of righteousness refers to the solid food. "The good word" mentioned in 6:5 is "the word of the beginning of Christ" (6:1). But the word of righteousness is deeper than the rudiments of the beginning of the oracles of God because it embodies the deeper thought of God's justice and righteousness in His dispensational and governmental dealings with His people. This word is more difficult to discriminate than the word of grace (Acts 14:3; 20:32) and the word of life (Phil. 2:16). (*Elders' Training, Book 6: The Crucial Points of the Truth in Paul's Epistles*, p. 127)

Today's Reading

When the righteous requirements of the law are fulfilled in us because we walk according to the Spirit, then we have righteousness. Righteousness...signifies the expression of God, His image. When we have righteousness, we have the expression of the God we serve and worship. Day by day, we need to walk according to the Spirit of life so that we may fulfill the righteousness of the law [Rom. 8:2, 4]. This is equal to being conformed to the image of God's Son [v. 29].

Romans 14:17 says, "For the kingdom of God is not eating and drinking, but righteousness and peace and joy in the Holy Spirit." In this verse Paul gives us another aspect of righteousness. In Romans 8 we have righteousness related to the Spirit of life and issuing in the image of the Son of God. But in Romans 14:17

righteousness is related to the kingdom of God. In this chapter the kingdom of God denotes the church life....The church life is the kingdom of God, and the kingdom of God is righteousness. In the Old Testament righteousness is often synonymous with the kingdom. Therefore, righteousness is related to government, administration, regulation, and rule. Righteousness means that things are set up and maintained in good order. Where there is righteousness, everything is headed up in a proper way. This is the kingdom.

Righteousness first issues in the image of God. Then righteousness establishes the kingdom of God....Both the image and the kingdom are based on righteousness.

Revelation 19:7 and 8 say, "Let us rejoice and exult, and let us give the glory to Him, for the marriage of the Lamb has come, and His wife has made herself ready. And it was given to her that she should be clothed in fine linen, bright and clean; for the fine linen is the righteousnesses of the saints." The bride here refers to redeemed and transformed tripartite mankind. This bride will wear white linen, which is the righteousnesses of the saints.

If we would have a share in this bride, who is adorned with bright, shining, pure righteousness, we need to adorn ourselves with righteousness. Day by day we need to prepare bright linen clothing to cover ourselves. This is our daily righteousness.

How can we produce such a garment of righteousness? We produce it by walking daily according to the Spirit of life and by having a life that is a life of the Spirit. If we prepare our wedding garment day by day, month by month, and year by year by living such a life in the Spirit, we shall not be found naked when the Lord comes. Instead, at His coming, we shall be wearing a bright, pure wedding garment. (*Life-study of 2 Corinthians*, pp. 257-260)

Further Reading: Elders' Training, Book 6: The Crucial Points of the Truth in Paul's Epistles, ch. 10; God's New Testament Economy, msg. 9; The Scriptural Way to Meet and to Serve for the Building Up of the Body of Christ, ch. 18; Life-study of Hebrews, msg. 29; Life-study of 2 Corinthians, msgs. 29-30, 37

Enlightenment and inspiration: _____

_____

_____

_____

Morning Nourishment

2 Cor. Him who did not know sin He made sin on our
5:21 behalf that we might become the righteousness of
God in Him.

2 Pet. And did not spare the ancient world but guarded
2:5 Noah, a herald of righteousness, with seven others,
when He brought a flood upon the world of the
ungodly.

As a result of experiencing the Spirit living and working
within us, we become righteous. Spontaneously our inner being
is transparent, crystal clear, and we know the heart of God.
Immediately, without effort, we know the mind of the Lord
and have a clear understanding concerning His will and work.
Then what we do is according to the Lord's mind and will. This
is righteousness.

Many Christians have the concept that when we do something wrong, we are not right with God. This concept of righteousness is too superficial. Even when we do not do anything
wrong we still may not be right with God, for our being may
not be in the mind and will of the Lord. Apparently we are not
wrong in any way; however, our entire being may be far short
of being right with God. We may not be according to the Lord's
mind, and what we are doing may not be His will. As long as
we are not doing God's will, we are not right. Instead we are
wasting our lives and everything the Lord has given us. (*Life-
study of 2 Corinthians*, p. 242)

Today's Reading

Suppose a young person at school does not do anything
wrong. But he does not study properly. Furthermore, when he
sits in class, he is absent-minded. Even though he may not do
anything wrong, he is more wrong than other students. Outwardly he may not be wrong, but inwardly his whole being
is wrong. In the same principle, outwardly many saints are
not wrong in anything. Actually, their being is not in the will
of the Lord. This understanding of being right with God is not

merely according to doctrine, but even the more, it is according to experience.

If you are infused and saturated by the life-giving Spirit, your inner being will become transparent. Then you will know what is in the Lord's mind. You will also understand what the will of the Lord is. Spontaneously, you will be in His will and do His will. As a result, you become right with Him. Moreover, you will realize how you should act toward others and even how you should deal with your material possessions. Then you will become a righteous person, one who is right in small things as well as in great things, one who is right with God, with others, and with himself. This is a person who expresses God, for his righteousness is the image of God, God expressed. (*Life-study of 2 Corinthians,* pp. 242-243)

In His old administrative arrangement God judged the ungodly generation with the flood and delivered Noah and his family out of the corrupted generation....Noah was a herald of righteousness. To be righteous and godly or unrighteous and ungodly is crucial with respect to God's governmental judgment (2 Pet. 2:5-9). To be righteous is to be right with man before God, and to be godly is to express God before man. This was the manner of life Noah lived, which saved him from God's governmental judgment according to His righteousness.

Noah did not preach the gospel; he preached God's righteousness over against the corruption of his generation. Peter speaks of righteousness here because his emphasis is on God's government. Noah's preaching of righteousness was related to God's government. God told Noah that He would wipe out the world and that Noah should preach righteousness to his generation. God exercised His judgment upon that corrupted generation by bringing a flood upon the world of the ungodly. (*The Conclusion of the New Testament,* p. 149)

Further Reading: Life-study of 2 Corinthians, msgs. 27-28; The Conclusion of the New Testament, msg. 14

Enlightenment and inspiration: _____

_____

_____

_____

Morning Nourishment

Gen. All these are the twelve tribes of Israel, and this is
49:28 what their father spoke to them when he blessed
them; he blessed them, each one according to his
blessing.
47:7 And Joseph brought in Jacob his father and set him
before Pharaoh, and Jacob blessed Pharaoh.
John He who believes into Me, as the Scripture said, out of
7:38 his innermost being shall flow rivers of living water.

The strongest manifestation of Jacob's maturity in life is the
fact that Jacob blessed everyone, including Pharaoh (Gen. 47:7, 10),
Jacob's two grandsons (ch. 48), and his own twelve sons (49:1-28).
Jacob's supplanting hands became blessing hands (48:14-16).
Maturity in life is a matter of being filled with God as life, and
blessing is the overflow of life, the overflow of God through the
maturity in life. To bless others is to bring them into the presence
of God and to bring God into them as grace, love, and fellowship
that they may enjoy the Triune God—the Father, the Son, and the
Spirit (14:18-19; Num. 6:23-27; 2 Cor. 13:14). That Jacob blessed
Pharaoh indicates that he was greater than Pharaoh (Heb. 7:7).
(Genesis 47:7, footnote 1)

Today's Reading

[Jacob's maturity in life is manifested in] his prophesying with
blessing (Gen. 49:1-28). Although we are familiar with what it
means to prophesy, we may not be familiar with prophesying with
blessing. Genesis 49 is the only chapter that reveals this matter.

The prophesying in chapter forty-nine is a manifestation of
maturity, for our speaking always reveals where we are and
how mature we are....A young man speaks like a young man, a
middle-aged person like a middle-aged person, and a grandfather
like a grandfather. Hence, our speaking not only represents our
age, but also the kind of person we are.

Because of his maturity, Jacob's word in chapter forty-nine
was very weighty. Every word he uttered here became a prophecy....In Genesis 49 we see a person who has fully matured. This

man does not speak in a shallow, light, idle manner; he speaks in a way that is full of life and maturity. This indicates that our growth in life will be manifested in our speaking.

In order to prophesy with blessing, we must fulfill four requirements. The first requirement is to know God, the desire of God's heart, and the purpose of God....The second requirement is to know people, to know the actual situation of every person involved....Jacob had a proper understanding of his sons. He knew their deeds, their situations, and their condition. Jacob was an expert in knowing people. He had a spiritual x-ray.

Although we may know God, God's heart, and God's purpose and although we may know the situation of others, we shall still not be able to bless them if we are poor....Jacob, however, was full of riches. Because he had no lack of riches, he could bless others.... In addition,...we need a strong, active spirit. Jacob's word in this chapter was spoken as he was dying....Although Jacob was dying physically, he was vigorous spiritually. In his body he was dying, but in his spirit he was strong and active. Therefore, in order to prophesy with blessing, we must have the knowledge of God, the knowledge of people and their situations, the riches of God, and a strong spirit. (*Life-study of Genesis,* pp. 1231, 1234-1236)

The Triune God is a speaking God (Heb. 1:1-2)....He has been speaking through the prophets in different ways, and now He is still speaking through His Son. His Son, Jesus Christ, is the Word of God. When someone is ministering the word of God in the Spirit, apparently it is he who is speaking, but actually it is Christ, the Son of God, speaking. This minister of the word is nothing, but out of his lips something comes from One who is everything. God is still speaking today. (*The Triune God's Revelation and His Move,* pp. 3-4)

Further Reading: Life-study of Genesis, msg. 97; *The Triune God's Revelation and His Move,* msg. 1; *The Practice of the Church Life according to the God-ordained Way,* ch. 4; *The Ministry of God's Word,* ch. 1*

Enlightenment and inspiration: _____

_____

_____

_____

Hymns, #869

1   Ere we depart, we praise Thee, Lord, again
For Thy dear presence and Thy living word;
We are attracted by Thy preciousness,
Our hearts incline to Thee through what we've heard.

2   Thy word is spirit and is life to us,
By it we're nourished, growing, Lord, in Thee;
Thus to Thine image we may be transformed,
With Thy full measure to maturity.

3   Impart Thyself to us, Lord, more and more,
And make us in the spirit walk and move,
That we be kept in fellowship with Thee,
Until we meet again, Thy grace to prove.

Composition for prophecy with main point and sub-points: _____

_____
_____
_____
_____
_____
_____
_____
_____
_____
_____
_____
_____
_____
_____
_____
_____
_____
_____
_____
_____
_____
_____
_____
_____
_____
_____
_____
_____
_____
_____
_____
_____
_____
_____
_____
_____

Reading Schedule for the Recovery Version of the Old Testament with Footnotes

Wk.	Lord's Day	Monday	Tuesday	Wednesday	Thursday	Friday	Saturday
1	☐ Gen 1:1-5	☐ 1:6-23	☐ 1:24-31	☐ 2:1-9	☐ 2:10-25	☐ 3:1-13	☐ 3:14-24
2	☐ 4:1-26	☐ 5:1-32	☐ 6:1-22	☐ 7:1—8:3	☐ 8:4-22	☐ 9:1-29	☐ 10:1-32
3	☐ 11:1-32	☐ 12:1-20	☐ 13:1-18	☐ 14:1-24	☐ 15:1-21	☐ 16:1-16	☐ 17:1-27
4	☐ 18:1-33	☐ 19:1-38	☐ 20:1-18	☐ 21:1-34	☐ 22:1-24	☐ 23:1—24:27	☐ 24:28-67
5	☐ 25:1-34	☐ 26:1-35	☐ 27:1-46	☐ 28:1-22	☐ 29:1-35	☐ 30:1-43	☐ 31:1-55
6	☐ 32:1-32	☐ 33:1—34:31	☐ 35:1-29	☐ 36:1-43	☐ 37:1-36	☐ 38:1—39:23	☐ 40:1—41:13
7	☐ 41:14-57	☐ 42:1-38	☐ 43:1-34	☐ 44:1-34	☐ 45:1-28	☐ 46:1-34	☐ 47:1-31
8	☐ 48:1-22	☐ 49:1-15	☐ 49:16-33	☐ 50:1-26	☐ Exo 1:1-22	☐ 2:1-25	☐ 3:1-22
9	☐ 4:1-31	☐ 5:1-23	☐ 6:1-30	☐ 7:1-25	☐ 8:1-32	☐ 9:1-35	☐ 10:1-29
10	☐ 11:1-10	☐ 12:1-14	☐ 12:15-36	☐ 12:37-51	☐ 13:1-22	☐ 14:1-31	☐ 15:1-27
11	☐ 16:1-36	☐ 17:1-16	☐ 18:1-27	☐ 19:1-25	☐ 20:1-26	☐ 21:1-36	☐ 22:1-31
12	☐ 23:1-33	☐ 24:1-18	☐ 25:1-22	☐ 25:23-40	☐ 26:1-14	☐ 26:15-37	☐ 27:1-21
13	☐ 28:1-21	☐ 28:22-43	☐ 29:1-21	☐ 29:22-46	☐ 30:1-10	☐ 30:11-38	☐ 31:1-17
14	☐ 31:18—32:35	☐ 33:1-23	☐ 34:1-35	☐ 35:1-35	☐ 36:1-38	☐ 37:1-29	☐ 38:1-31
15	☐ 39:1-43	☐ 40:1-38	☐ Lev 1:1-17	☐ 2:1-16	☐ 3:1-17	☐ 4:1-35	☐ 5:1-19
16	☐ 6:1-30	☐ 7:1-38	☐ 8:1-36	☐ 9:1-24	☐ 10:1-20	☐ 11:1-47	☐ 12:1-8
17	☐ 13:1-28	☐ 13:29-59	☐ 14:1-18	☐ 14:19-32	☐ 14:33-57	☐ 15:1-33	☐ 16:1-17
18	☐ 16:18-34	☐ 17:1-16	☐ 18:1-30	☐ 19:1-37	☐ 20:1-27	☐ 21:1-24	☐ 22:1-33
19	☐ 23:1-22	☐ 23:23-44	☐ 24:1-23	☐ 25:1-23	☐ 25:24-55	☐ 26:1-24	☐ 26:25-46
20	☐ 27:1-34	☐ Num 1:1-54	☐ 2:1-34	☐ 3:1-51	☐ 4:1-49	☐ 5:1-31	☐ 6:1-27
21	☐ 7:1-41	☐ 7:42-88	☐ 7:89—8:26	☐ 9:1-23	☐ 10:1-36	☐ 11:1-35	☐ 12:1—13:33
22	☐ 14:1-45	☐ 15:1-41	☐ 16:1-50	☐ 17:1—18:7	☐ 18:8-32	☐ 19:1-22	☐ 20:1-29
23	☐ 21:1-35	☐ 22:1-41	☐ 23:1-30	☐ 24:1-25	☐ 25:1-18	☐ 26:1-65	☐ 27:1-23
24	☐ 28:1-31	☐ 29:1-40	☐ 30:1—31:24	☐ 31:25-54	☐ 32:1-42	☐ 33:1-56	☐ 34:1-29
25	☐ 35:1-34	☐ 36:1-13	☐ Deut 1:1-46	☐ 2:1-37	☐ 3:1-29	☐ 4:1-49	☐ 5:1-33
26	☐ 6:1—7:26	☐ 8:1-20	☐ 9:1-29	☐ 10:1-22	☐ 11:1-32	☐ 12:1-32	☐ 13:1—14:21

Reading Schedule for the Recovery Version of the Old Testament with Footnotes

Wk.	Lord's Day	Monday	Tuesday	Wednesday	Thursday	Friday	Saturday
27	□ 14:22—15:23	□ 16:1-22	□ 17:1—18:8	□ 18:9—19:21	□ 20:1—21:17	□ 21:18—22:30	□ 23:1-25
28	□ 24:1-22	□ 25:1-19	□ 26:1-19	□ 27:1-26	□ 28:1-68	□ 29:1-29	□ 30:1—31:29
29	□ 31:30—32:52	□ 33:1-29	□ 34:1-12	□ Josh 1:1-18	□ 2:1-24	□ 3:1-17	□ 4:1-24
30	□ 5:1-15	□ 6:1-27	□ 7:1-26	□ 8:1-35	□ 9:1-27	□ 10:1-43	□ 11:1—12:24
31	□ 13:1-33	□ 14:1—15:63	□ 16:1—18:28	□ 19:1-51	□ 20:1—21:45	□ 22:1-34	□ 23:1—24:33
32	□ Judg 1:1-36	□ 2:1-23	□ 3:1-31	□ 4:1-24	□ 5:1-31	□ 6:1-40	□ 7:1-25
33	□ 8:1-35	□ 9:1-57	□ 10:1—11:40	□ 12:1—13:25	□ 14:1—15:20	□ 16:1-31	□ 17:1—18:31
34	□ 19:1-30	□ 20:1-48	□ 21:1-25	□ Ruth 1:1-22	□ 2:1-23	□ 3:1-18	□ 4:1-22
35	□ 1 Sam 1:1-28	□ 2:1-36	□ 3:1—4:22	□ 5:1—6:21	□ 7:1—8:22	□ 9:1-27	□ 10:1—11:15
36	□ 12:1—13:23	□ 14:1-52	□ 15:1-35	□ 16:1-23	□ 17:1-58	□ 18:1-30	□ 19:1-24
37	□ 20:1-42	□ 21:1—22:23	□ 23:1—24:22	□ 25:1-44	□ 26:1-25	□ 27:1—28:25	□ 29:1—30:31
38	□ 31:1-13	□ 2 Sam 1:1-27	□ 2:1-32	□ 3:1-39	□ 4:1—5:25	□ 6:1-23	□ 7:1-29
39	□ 8:1—9:13	□ 10:1—11:27	□ 12:1-31	□ 13:1-39	□ 14:1-33	□ 15:1—16:23	□ 17:1—18:33
40	□ 19:1-43	□ 20:1—21:22	□ 22:1-51	□ 23:1-39	□ 24:1-25	□ 1 Kings 1:1-19	□ 1:20-53
41	□ 2:1-46	□ 3:1-28	□ 4:1-34	□ 5:1—6:38	□ 7:1-22	□ 7:23-51	□ 8:1-36
42	□ 8:37-66	□ 9:1-28	□ 10:1-29	□ 11:1-43	□ 12:1-33	□ 13:1-34	□ 14:1-31
43	□ 15:1-34	□ 16:1—17:24	□ 18:1-46	□ 19:1-21	□ 20:1-43	□ 21:1—22:53	□ 2 Kings 1:1-18
44	□ 2:1—3:27	□ 4:1-44	□ 5:1—6:33	□ 7:1-20	□ 8:1-29	□ 9:1-37	□ 10:1-36
45	□ 11:1—12:21	□ 13:1—14:29	□ 15:1-38	□ 16:1-20	□ 17:1-41	□ 18:1-37	□ 19:1-37
46	□ 20:1—21:26	□ 22:1-20	□ 23:1-37	□ 24:1—25:30	□ 1 Chron 1:1-54	□ 2:1—3:24	□ 4:1—5:26
47	□ 6:1-81	□ 7:1-40	□ 8:1-40	□ 9:1-44	□ 10:1—11:47	□ 12:1-40	□ 13:1—14:17
48	□ 15:1—16:43	□ 17:1-27	□ 18:1—19:19	□ 20:1—21:30	□ 22:1—23:32	□ 24:1—25:31	□ 26:1-32
49	□ 27:1-34	□ 28:1—29:30	□ 2 Chron 1:1-17	□ 2:1—3:17	□ 4:1—5:14	□ 6:1-42	□ 7:1—8:18
50	□ 9:1—10:19	□ 11:1—12:16	□ 13:1—15:19	□ 16:1—17:19	□ 18:1—19:11	□ 20:1-37	□ 21:1—22:12
51	□ 23:1—24:27	□ 25:1—26:23	□ 27:1—28:27	□ 29:1-36	□ 30:1—31:21	□ 32:1-33	□ 33:1—34:33
52	□ 35:1—36:23	□ Ezra 1:1-11	□ 2:1-70	□ 3:1—4:24	□ 5:1—6:22	□ 7:1-28	□ 8:1-36

Reading Schedule for the Recovery Version of the Old Testament with Footnotes

Wk.	Lord's Day	Monday	Tuesday	Wednesday	Thursday	Friday	Saturday
53	□ 9:1—10:44	□ Neh 1:1-11	□ 2:1—3:32	□ 4:1—5:19	□ 6:1-19	□ 7:1-73	□ 8:1-18
54	□ 9:1-20	□ 9:21-38	□ 10:1—11:36	□ 12:1-47	□ 13:1-31	□ Esth 1:1-22	□ 2:1—3:15
55	□ 4:1—5:14	□ 6:1—7:10	□ 8:1-17	□ 9:1—10:3	□ Job 1:1-22	□ 2:1—3:26	□ 4:1—5:27
56	□ 6:1—7:21	□ 8:1—9:35	□ 10:1—11:20	□ 12:1—13:28	□ 14:1—15:35	□ 16:1—17:16	□ 18:1—19:29
57	□ 20:1—21:34	□ 22:1—23:17	□ 24:1—25:6	□ 26:1—27:23	□ 28:1—29:25	□ 30:1—31:40	□ 32:1—33:33
58	□ 34:1—35:16	□ 36:1-33	□ 37:1-24	□ 38:1-41	□ 39:1-30	□ 40:1-24	□ 41:1-34
59	□ 42:1-17	□ Psa 1:1-6	□ 2:1—3:8	□ 4:1—6:10	□ 7:1—8:9	□ 9:1—10:18	□ 11:1—15:5
60	□ 16:1—17:15	□ 18:1-50	□ 19:1—21:13	□ 22:1-31	□ 23:1—24:10	□ 25:1—27:14	□ 28:1—30:12
61	□ 31:1—32:11	□ 33:1—34:22	□ 35:1—36:12	□ 37:1-40	□ 38:1—39:13	□ 40:1—41:13	□ 42:1—43:5
62	□ 44:1-26	□ 45:1-17	□ 46:1—48:14	□ 49:1—50:23	□ 51:1—52:9	□ 53:1—55:23	□ 56:1—58:11
63	□ 59:1—61:8	□ 62:1—64:10	□ 65:1—67:7	□ 68:1-35	□ 69:1—70:5	□ 71:1—72:20	□ 73:1—74:23
64	□ 75:1—77:20	□ 78:1-72	□ 79:1—81:16	□ 82:1—84:12	□ 85:1—87:7	□ 88:1—89:52	□ 90:1—91:16
65	□ 92:1—94:23	□ 95:1—97:12	□ 98:1—101:8	□ 102:1—103:22	□ 104:1—105:45	□ 106:1-48	□ 107:1-43
66	□ 108:1—109:31	□ 110:1—112:10	□ 113:1—115:18	□ 116:1—118:29	□ 119:1-32	□ 119:33-72	□ 119:73-120
67	□ 119:121-176	□ 120:1—124:8	□ 125:1—128:6	□ 129:1—132:18	□ 133:1—135:21	□ 136:1—138:8	□ 139:1—140:13
68	□ 141:1—144:15	□ 145:1—147:20	□ 148:1—150:6	□ Prov 1:1-33	□ 2:1—3:35	□ 4:1—5:23	□ 6:1-35
69	□ 7:1—8:36	□ 9:1—10:32	□ 11:1—12:28	□ 13:1—14:35	□ 15:1-33	□ 16:1-33	□ 17:1-28
70	□ 18:1-24	□ 19:1—20:30	□ 21:1—22:29	□ 23:1-35	□ 24:1—25:28	□ 26:1—27:27	□ 28:1—29:27
71	□ 30:1-33	□ 31:1-31	□ Eccl 1:1-18	□ 2:1—3:22	□ 4:1—5:20	□ 6:1—7:29	□ 8:1—9:18
72	□ 10:1—11:10	□ 12:1-14	□ S.S 1:1-8	□ 1:9-17	□ 2:1-17	□ 3:1-11	□ 4:1-8
73	□ 4:9-16	□ 5:1-16	□ 6:1-13	□ 7:1-13	□ 8:1-14	□ Isa 1:1-11	□ 1:12-31
74	□ 2:1-22	□ 3:1-26	□ 4:1-6	□ 5:1-30	□ 6:1-13	□ 7:1-25	□ 8:1-22
75	□ 9:1-21	□ 10:1-34	□ 11:1—12:6	□ 13:1-22	□ 14:1-14	□ 14:15-32	□ 15:1—16:14
76	□ 17:1—18:7	□ 19:1-25	□ 20:1—21:17	□ 22:1-25	□ 23:1-18	□ 24:1-23	□ 25:1-12
77	□ 26:1-21	□ 27:1-13	□ 28:1-29	□ 29:1-24	□ 30:1-33	□ 31:1—32:20	□ 33:1-24
78	□ 34:1-17	□ 35:1-10	□ 36:1-22	□ 37:1-38	□ 38:1—39:8	□ 40:1-31	□ 41:1-29

Reading Schedule for the Recovery Version of the Old Testament with Footnotes

Wk.	Lord's Day	Monday	Tuesday	Wednesday	Thursday	Friday	Saturday
79	☐ 42:1-25	☐ 43:1-28	☐ 44:1-28	☐ 45:1-25	☐ 46:1-13	☐ 47:1-15	☐ 48:1-22
80	☐ 49:1-13	☐ 49:14-26	☐ 50:1—51:23	☐ 52:1-15	☐ 53:1-12	☐ 54:1-17	☐ 55:1-13
81	☐ 56:1-12	☐ 57:1-21	☐ 58:1-14	☐ 59:1-21	☐ 60:1-22	☐ 61:1-11	☐ 62:1-12
82	☐ 63:1-19	☐ 64:1-12	☐ 65:1-25	☐ 66:1-24	☐ Jer 1:1-19	☐ 2:1-19	☐ 2:20-37
83	☐ 3:1-25	☐ 4:1-31	☐ 5:1-31	☐ 6:1-30	☐ 7:1-34	☐ 8:1-22	☐ 9:1-26
84	☐ 10:1-25	☐ 11:1—12:17	☐ 13:1-27	☐ 14:1-22	☐ 15:1-21	☐ 16:1—17:27	☐ 18:1-23
85	☐ 19:1—20:18	☐ 21:1—22:30	☐ 23:1-40	☐ 24:1—25:38	☐ 26:1—27:22	☐ 28:1—29:32	☐ 30:1-24
86	☐ 31:1-23	☐ 31:24-40	☐ 32:1-44	☐ 33:1-26	☐ 34:1-22	☐ 35:1-19	☐ 36:1-32
87	☐ 37:1-21	☐ 38:1-28	☐ 39:1—40:16	☐ 41:1—42:22	☐ 43:1—44:30	☐ 45:1—46:28	☐ 47:1—48:16
88	☐ 48:17-47	☐ 49:1-22	☐ 49:23-39	☐ 50:1-27	☐ 50:28-46	☐ 51:1-27	☐ 51:28-64
89	☐ 52:1-34	☐ Lam 1:1-22	☐ 2:1-22	☐ 3:1-39	☐ 3:40-66	☐ 4:1-22	☐ 5:1-22
90	☐ Ezek 1:1-14	☐ 1:15-28	☐ 2:1—3:27	☐ 4:1—5:17	☐ 6:1—7:27	☐ 8:1—9:11	☐ 10:1—11:25
91	☐ 12:1—13:23	☐ 14:1—15:8	☐ 16:1-63	☐ 17:1—18:32	☐ 19:1-14	☐ 20:1-49	☐ 21:1-32
92	☐ 22:1-31	☐ 23:1-49	☐ 24:1-27	☐ 25:1—26:21	☐ 27:1-36	☐ 28:1-26	☐ 29:1—30:26
93	☐ 31:1—32:32	☐ 33:1-33	☐ 34:1-31	☐ 35:1—36:21	☐ 36:22-38	☐ 37:1-28	☐ 38:1—39:29
94	☐ 40:1-27	☐ 40:28-49	☐ 41:1-26	☐ 42:1—43:27	☐ 44:1-31	☐ 45:1-25	☐ 46:1-24
95	☐ 47:1-23	☐ 48:1-35	☐ Dan 1:1-21	☐ 2:1-30	☐ 2:31-49	☐ 3:1-30	☐ 4:1-37
96	☐ 5:1-31	☐ 6:1-28	☐ 7:1-12	☐ 7:13-28	☐ 8:1-27	☐ 9:1-27	☐ 10:1-21
97	☐ 11:1-22	☐ 11:23-45	☐ 12:1-13	☐ Hosea 1:1-11	☐ 2:1-23	☐ 3:1—4:19	☐ 5:1-15
98	☐ 6:1-11	☐ 7:1-16	☐ 8:1-14	☐ 9:1-17	☐ 10:1-15	☐ 11:1-12	☐ 12:1-14
99	☐ 13:1—14:9	☐ Joel 1:1-20	☐ 2:1-16	☐ 2:17-32	☐ 3:1-21	☐ Amos 1:1-15	☐ 2:1-16
100	☐ 3:1-15	☐ 4:1—5:27	☐ 6:1—7:17	☐ 8:1—9:15	☐ Obad 1-21	☐ Jonah 1:1-17	☐ 2:1—4:11
101	☐ Micah 1:1-16	☐ 2:1—3:12	☐ 4:1—5:15	☐ 6:1—7:20	☐ Nahum 1:1-15	☐ 2:1—3:19	☐ Hab 1:1-17
102	☐ 2:1-20	☐ 3:1-19	☐ Zeph 1:1-18	☐ 2:1-15	☐ 3:1-20	☐ Hag 1:1-15	☐ 2:1-23
103	☐ Zech 1:1-21	☐ 2:1-13	☐ 3:1-10	☐ 4:1-14	☐ 5:1—6:15	☐ 7:1—8:23	☐ 9:1-17
104	☐ 10:1—11:17	☐ 12:1—13:9	☐ 14:1-21	☐ Mal 1:1-14	☐ 2:1-17	☐ 3:1-18	☐ 4:1-6

Reading Schedule for the Recovery Version of the New Testament with Footnotes

Wk.	Lord's Day	Monday	Tuesday	Wednesday	Thursday	Friday	Saturday
1	Matt 1:1-2	1:3-7	1:8-17	1:18-25	2:1-23	3:1-6	3:7-17
2	4:1-11	4:12-25	5:1-4	5:5-12	5:13-20	5:21-26	5:27-48
3	6:1-8	6:9-18	6:19-34	7:1-12	7:13-29	8:1-13	8:14-22
4	8:23-34	9:1-13	9:14-17	9:18-34	9:35—10:5	10:6-25	10:26-42
5	11:1-15	11:16-30	12:1-14	12:15-32	12:33-42	12:43—13:2	13:3-12
6	13:13-30	13:31-43	13:44-58	14:1-13	14:14-21	14:22-36	15:1-20
7	15:21-31	15:32-39	16:1-12	16:13-20	16:21-28	17:1-13	17:14-27
8	18:1-14	18:15-22	18:23-35	19:1-15	19:16-30	20:1-16	20:17-34
9	21:1-11	21:12-22	21:23-32	21:33-46	22:1-22	22:23-33	22:34-46
10	23:1-12	23:13-39	24:1-14	24:15-31	24:32-51	25:1-13	25:14-30
11	25:31-46	26:1-16	26:17-35	26:36-46	26:47-64	26:65-75	27:1-26
12	27:27-44	27:45-56	27:57—28:15	28:16-20	Mark 1:1	1:2-6	1:7-13
13	1:14-28	1:29-45	2:1-12	2:13-28	3:1-19	3:20-35	4:1-25
14	4:26-41	5:1-20	5:21-43	6:1-29	6:30-56	7:1-23	7:24-37
15	8:1-26	8:27—9:1	9:2-29	9:30-50	10:1-16	10:17-34	10:35-52
16	11:1-16	11:17-33	12:1-27	12:28-44	13:1-13	13:14-37	14:1-26
17	14:27-52	14:53-72	15:1-15	15:16-47	16:1-8	16:9-20	Luke 1:1-4
18	1:5-25	1:26-46	1:47-56	1:57-80	2:1-8	2:9-20	2:21-39
19	2:40-52	3:1-20	3:21-38	4:1-13	4:14-30	4:31-44	5:1-26
20	5:27—6:16	6:17-38	6:39-49	7:1-17	7:18-23	7:24-35	7:36-50
21	8:1-15	8:16-25	8:26-39	8:40-56	9:1-17	9:18-26	9:27-36
22	9:37-50	9:51-62	10:1-11	10:12-24	10:25-37	10:38-42	11:1-13
23	11:14-26	11:27-36	11:37-54	12:1-12	12:13-21	12:22-34	12:35-48
24	12:49-59	13:1-9	13:10-17	13:18-30	13:31—14:6	14:7-14	14:15-24
25	14:25-35	15:1-10	15:11-21	15:22-32	16:1-13	16:14-22	16:23-31
26	17:1-19	17:20-37	18:1-14	18:15-30	18:31-43	19:1-10	19:11-27

Reading Schedule for the Recovery Version of the New Testament with Footnotes

Wk.	Lord's Day	Monday	Tuesday	Wednesday	Thursday	Friday	Saturday
27	□ Luke 19:28-48	□ 20:1-19	□ 20:20-38	□ 20:39—21:4	□ 21:5-27	□ 21:28-38	□ 22:1-20
28	□ 22:21-38	□ 22:39-54	□ 22:55-71	□ 23:1-43	□ 23:44-56	□ 24:1-12	□ 24:13-35
29	□ 24:36-53	□ John 1:1-13	□ 1:14-18	□ 1:19-34	□ 1:35-51	□ 2:1-11	□ 2:12-22
30	□ 2:23—3:13	□ 3:14-21	□ 3:22-36	□ 4:1-14	□ 4:15-26	□ 4:27-42	□ 4:43-54
31	□ 5:1-16	□ 5:17-30	□ 5:31-47	□ 6:1-15	□ 6:16-31	□ 6:32-51	□ 6:52-71
32	□ 7:1-9	□ 7:10-24	□ 7:25-36	□ 7:37-52	□ 7:53—8:11	□ 8:12-27	□ 8:28-44
33	□ 8:45-59	□ 9:1-13	□ 9:14-34	□ 9:35—10:9	□ 10:10-30	□ 10:31—11:4	□ 11:5-22
34	□ 11:23-40	□ 11:41-57	□ 12:1-11	□ 12:12-24	□ 12:25-36	□ 12:37-50	□ 13:1-11
35	□ 13:12-30	□ 13:31-38	□ 14:1-6	□ 14:7-20	□ 14:21-31	□ 15:1-11	□ 15:12-27
36	□ 16:1-15	□ 16:16-33	□ 17:1-5	□ 17:6-13	□ 17:14-24	□ 17:25—18:11	□ 18:12-27
37	□ 18:28-40	□ 19:1-16	□ 19:17-30	□ 19:31-42	□ 20:1-13	□ 20:14-18	□ 20:19-22
38	□ 20:23-31	□ 21:1-14	□ 21:15-22	□ 21:23-25	□ Acts 1:1-8	□ 1:9-14	□ 1:15-26
39	□ 2:1-13	□ 2:14-21	□ 2:22-36	□ 2:37-41	□ 2:42-47	□ 3:1-18	□ 3:19—4:22
40	□ 4:23-37	□ 5:1-16	□ 5:17-32	□ 5:33-42	□ 6:1—7:1	□ 7:2-29	□ 7:30-60
41	□ 8:1-13	□ 8:14-25	□ 8:26-40	□ 9:1-19	□ 9:20-43	□ 10:1-16	□ 10:17-33
42	□ 10:34-48	□ 11:1-18	□ 11:19-30	□ 12:1-25	□ 13:1-12	□ 13:13-43	□ 13:44—14:5
43	□ 14:6-28	□ 15:1-12	□ 15:13-34	□ 15:35—16:5	□ 16:6-18	□ 16:19-40	□ 17:1-18
44	□ 17:19-34	□ 18:1-17	□ 18:18-28	□ 19:1-20	□ 19:21-41	□ 20:1-12	□ 20:13-38
45	□ 21:1-14	□ 21:15-26	□ 21:27-40	□ 22:1-21	□ 22:22-29	□ 22:30—23:11	□ 23:12-15
46	□ 23:16-30	□ 23:31—24:21	□ 24:22—25:5	□ 25:6-27	□ 26:1-13	□ 26:14-32	□ 27:1-26
47	□ 27:27—28:10	□ 28:11-22	□ 28:23-31	□ Rom 1:1-2	□ 1:3-7	□ 1:8-17	□ 1:18-25
48	□ 1:26—2:10	□ 2:11-29	□ 3:1-20	□ 3:21-31	□ 4:1-12	□ 4:13-25	□ 5:1-11
49	□ 5:12-17	□ 5:18—6:5	□ 6:6-11	□ 6:12-23	□ 7:1-12	□ 7:13-25	□ 8:1-2
50	□ 8:3-6	□ 8:7-13	□ 8:14-25	□ 8:26-39	□ 9:1-18	□ 9:19—10:3	□ 10:4-15
51	□ 10:16—11:10	□ 11:11-22	□ 11:23-36	□ 12:1-3	□ 12:4-21	□ 13:1-14	□ 14:1-12
52	□ 14:13-23	□ 15:1-13	□ 15:14-33	□ 16:1-5	□ 16:6-24	□ 16:25-27	□ 1 Cor 1:1-4

Reading Schedule for the Recovery Version of the New Testament with Footnotes

Wk.	Lord's Day	Monday	Tuesday	Wednesday	Thursday	Friday	Saturday
53	1 Cor 1:5-9	1:10-17	1:18-31	2:1-5	2:6-10	2:11-16	3:1-9
54	3:10-13	3:14-23	4:1-9	4:10-21	5:1-13	6:1-11	6:12-20
55	7:1-16	7:17-24	7:25-40	8:1-13	9:1-15	9:16-27	10:1-4
56	10:5-13	10:14-33	11:1-6	11:7-16	11:17-26	11:27-34	12:1-11
57	12:12-22	12:23-31	13:1-13	14:1-12	14:13-25	14:26-33	14:34-40
58	15:1-19	15:20-28	15:29-34	15:35-49	15:50-58	16:1-9	16:10-24
59	2 Cor 1:1-4	1:5-14	1:15-22	1:23—2:11	2:12-17	3:1-6	3:7-11
60	3:12-18	4:1-6	4:7-12	4:13-18	5:1-8	5:9-15	5:16-21
61	6:1-13	6:14—7:4	7:5-16	8:1-15	8:16-24	9:1-15	10:1-6
62	10:7-18	11:1-15	11:16-33	12:1-10	12:11-21	13:1-10	13:11-14
63	Gal 1:1-5	1:6-14	1:15-24	2:1-13	2:14-21	3:1-4	3:5-14
64	3:15-22	3:23-29	4:1-7	4:8-20	4:21-31	5:1-12	5:13-21
65	5:22-26	6:1-10	6:11-15	6:16-18	Eph 1:1-3	1:4-6	1:7-10
66	1:11-14	1:15-18	1:19-23	2:1-5	2:6-10	2:11-14	2:15-18
67	2:19-22	3:1-7	3:8-13	3:14-18	3:19-21	4:1-4	4:5-10
68	4:11-16	4:17-24	4:25-32	5:1-10	5:11-21	5:22-26	5:27-33
69	6:1-9	6:10-14	6:15-18	6:19-24	Phil 1:1-7	1:8-18	1:19-26
70	1:27—2:4	2:5-11	2:12-16	2:17-30	3:1-6`	3:7-11	3:12-16
71	3:17-21	4:1-9	4:10-23	Col 1:1-8	1:9-13	1:14-23	1:24-29
72	2:1-7	2:8-15	2:16-23	3:1-4	3:5-15	3:16-25	4:1-18
73	1 Thes 1:1-3	1:4-10	2:1-12	2:13—3:5	3:6-13	4:1-10	4:11—5:11
74	5:12-28	2 Thes 1:1-12	2:1-17	3:1-18	1 Tim 1:1-2	1:3-4	1:5-14
75	1:15-20	2:1-7	2:8-15	3:1-13	3:14—4:5	4:6-16	5:1-25
76	6:1-10	6:11-21	2 Tim 1:1-10	1:11-18	2:1-15	2:16-26	3:1-13
77	3:14—4:8	4:9-22	Titus 1:1-4	1:5-16	2:1-15	3:1-8	3:9-15
78	Philem 1:1-11	1:12-25	Heb 1:1-2	1:3-5	1:6-14	2:1-9	2:10-18

Reading Schedule for the Recovery Version of the New Testament with Footnotes

Wk.	Lord's Day	Monday	Tuesday	Wednesday	Thursday	Friday	Saturday
79	☐ Heb 3:1-6	☐ 3:7-19	☐ 4:1-9	☐ 4:10-13	☐ 4:14-16	☐ 5:1-10	☐ 5:11—6:3
80	☐ 6:4-8	☐ 6:9-20	☐ 7:1-10	☐ 7:11-28	☐ 8:1-6	☐ 8:7-13	☐ 9:1-4
81	☐ 9:5-14	☐ 9:15-28	☐ 10:1-18	☐ 10:19-28	☐ 10:29-39	☐ 11:1-6	☐ 11:7-19
82	☐ 11:20-31	☐ 11:32-40	☐ 12:1-2	☐ 12:3-13	☐ 12:14-17	☐ 12:18-26	☐ 12:27-29
83	☐ 13:1-7	☐ 13:8-12	☐ 13:13-15	☐ 13:16-25	☐ James 1:1-8	☐ 1:9-18	☐ 1:19-27
84	☐ 2:1-13	☐ 2:14-26	☐ 3:1-18	☐ 4:1-10	☐ 4:11-17	☐ 5:1-12	☐ 5:13-20
85	☐ 1 Pet 1:1-2	☐ 1:3-4	☐ 1:5	☐ 1:6-9	☐ 1:10-12	☐ 1:13-17	☐ 1:18-25
86	☐ 2:1-3	☐ 2:4-8	☐ 2:9-17	☐ 2:18-25	☐ 3:1-13	☐ 3:14-22	☐ 4:1-6
87	☐ 4:7-16	☐ 4:17-19	☐ 5:1-4	☐ 5:5-9	☐ 5:10-14	☐ 2 Pet 1:1-2	☐ 1:3-4
88	☐ 1:5-8	☐ 1:9-11	☐ 1:12-18	☐ 1:19-21	☐ 2:1-3	☐ 2:4-11	☐ 2:12-22
89	☐ 3:1-6	☐ 3:7-9	☐ 3:10-12	☐ 3:13-15	☐ 3:16	☐ 3:17-18	☐ 1 John 1:1-2
90	☐ 1:3-4	☐ 1:5	☐ 1:6	☐ 1:7	☐ 1:8-10	☐ 2:1-2	☐ 2:3-11
91	☐ 2:12-14	☐ 2:15-19	☐ 2:20-23	☐ 2:24-27	☐ 2:28-29	☐ 3:1-5	☐ 3:6-10
92	☐ 3:11-18	☐ 3:19-24	☐ 4:1-6	☐ 4:7-11	☐ 4:12-15	☐ 4:16—5:3	☐ 5:4-13
93	☐ 5:14-17	☐ 5:18-21	☐ 2 John 1:1-3	☐ 1:4-9	☐ 1:10-13	☐ 3 John 1:1-6	☐ 1:7-14
94	☐ Jude 1:1-4	☐ 1:5-10	☐ 1:11-19	☐ 1:20-25	☐ Rev 1:1-3	☐ 1:4-6	☐ 1:7-11
95	☐ 1:12-13	☐ 1:14-16	☐ 1:17-20	☐ 2:1-6	☐ 2:7	☐ 2:8-9	☐ 2:10-11
96	☐ 2:12-14	☐ 2:15-17	☐ 2:18-23	☐ 2:24-29	☐ 3:1-3	☐ 3:4-6	☐ 3:7-9
97	☐ 3:10-13	☐ 3:14-18	☐ 3:19-22	☐ 4:1-5	☐ 4:6-7	☐ 4:8-11	☐ 5:1-6
98	☐ 5:7-14	☐ 6:1-8	☐ 6:9-17	☐ 7:1-8	☐ 7:9-17	☐ 8:1-6	☐ 8:7-12
99	☐ 8:13—9:11	☐ 9:12-21	☐ 10:1-4	☐ 10:5-11	☐ 11:1-4	☐ 11:5-14	☐ 11:15-19
100	☐ 12:1-4	☐ 12:5-9	☐ 12:10-18	☐ 13:1-10	☐ 13:11-18	☐ 14:1-5	☐ 14:6-12
101	☐ 14:13-20	☐ 15:1-8	☐ 16:1-12	☐ 16:13-21	☐ 17:1-6	☐ 17:7-18	☐ 18:1-8
102	☐ 18:9—19:4	☐ 19:5-10	☐ 19:11-16	☐ 19:17-21	☐ 20:1-6	☐ 20:7-10	☐ 20:11-15
103	☐ 21:1	☐ 21:2	☐ 21:3-8	☐ 21:9-13	☐ 21:14-18	☐ 21:19-21	☐ 21:22-27
104	☐ 22:1	☐ 22:2	☐ 22:3-11	☐ 22:12-15	☐ 22:16-17	☐ 22:18-21	

Week 1 — Day 4 — Today's verses

John 3:34 For He whom God has sent speaks the words of God, for He gives the Spirit not by measure.

2 Cor. 4:13 And having the same spirit of faith according to that which is written, "I believed, therefore I spoke," we also believe, therefore we also speak.

_____
Date

Week 1 — Day 5 — Today's verses

1 Cor. 2:13 ...We speak, not in words taught by human wisdom but in words taught by the Spirit, interpreting spiritual things with spiritual _words_.

1 Thes. 2:4 But even as we have been approved by God to be entrusted with the gospel, so we speak, not as pleasing men but God, who proves our hearts.

_____
Date

Week 1 — Day 6 — Today's verses

John 12:49-50 ...I have not spoken from Myself; but the Father who sent Me, He Himself has given Me commandment, what to say and what to speak. And I know that His commandment is eternal life. The things therefore that I speak, even as the Father has said to Me, so I speak.

_____
Date

Week 1 — Day 1 — Today's verses

Heb. 11:3 By faith we understand that the universe has been framed by the word of God, so that what is seen has not come into being out of things which appear.

Matt. 4:4 But He answered and said, It is written, "Man shall not live on bread alone, but on every word that proceeds out through the mouth of God."

_____
Date

Week 1 — Day 2 — Today's verses

John 1:1 In the beginning was the Word, and the Word was with God, and the Word was God.

14 ...The Word became flesh and tabernacled among us...

18 No one has ever seen God; the only begotten Son, who is in the bosom of the Father, He has declared _Him_.

_____
Date

Week 1 — Day 3 — Today's verses

Heb. 1:1-3 God, having spoken of old in many portions and in many ways to the fathers in the prophets, has at the last of these days spoken to us in the Son...who, being the effulgence of His glory and the impress of His substance and upholding and bearing all things by the word of His power, having made purification of sins, sat down on the right hand of the Majesty on high.

_____
Date

Week 2 — Day 6

Today's verses

John 6:63 It is the Spirit who gives life; the flesh profits nothing; the words which I have spoken to you are spirit and are life.

1 Cor. 15:45 So also it is written, "The first man, Adam, became a living soul"; the last Adam *became* a life-giving Spirit.

_____
Date

Week 2 — Day 5

Today's verses

Eph. 6:17-18 And receive the helmet of salvation and the sword of the Spirit, which *Spirit* is the word of God, by means of all prayer and petition, praying at every time in spirit and watching unto this in all perseverance and petition concerning all the saints.

2 Cor. 3:17 And the Lord is the Spirit; and where the Spirit of the Lord is, there is freedom.

Rev. 19:13 And He is clothed with a garment dipped in blood; and His name is called the Word of God.

_____
Date

Week 2 — Day 4

Today's verses

Titus 3:5 Not out of works in righteousness which we did but according to His mercy He saved us, through the washing of regeneration and the renewing of the Holy Spirit.

Exo. 38:8 And he made the laver of bronze and its base of bronze from the mirrors of the serving women who served at the entrance of the Tent of Meeting.

_____
Date

Week 2 — Day 3

Today's verses

Exo. 30:18-21 You shall also make a laver of bronze for washing.... And Aaron and his sons shall wash their hands and their feet *with water* from it; when they go into the Tent of Meeting, they shall wash with water, that they may not die; or when they come near to the altar to minister, to burn an offering by fire to Jehovah, they shall wash their hands and their feet, that they may not die...

_____
Date

Week 2 — Day 2

Today's verses

Eph. 5:25-27 ...Christ also loved the church and gave Himself up for her that He might sanctify her, cleansing *her* by the washing of the water in the word, that He might present the church to Himself glorious, not having spot or wrinkle or any such things, but that she would be holy and without blemish.

_____
Date

Week 2 — Day 1

Today's verses

Eph. 5:26-27 That He might sanctify her, cleansing *her* by the washing of the water in the word, that He might present the church to Himself glorious, not having spot or wrinkle or any such things, but that she would be holy and without blemish.

6:17-18 And receive...the sword of the Spirit, which *Spirit* is the word of God, by means of all prayer and petition, praying at every time in spirit...

_____
Date

Week 3 — Day 4 — Today's verses

Col. 2:8 Beware that no one carries you off as spoil through his philosophy and empty deceit, according to the tradition of men, according to the elements of the world, and not according to Christ.

Col. 3:10-11 ...Put on the new man...where there cannot be Greek and Jew, circumcision and uncircumcision, barbarian, Scythian, slave, free man, but Christ is all and in all.

Date _____

Week 3 — Day 5 — Today's verses

John 6:63 It is the Spirit who gives life; the flesh profits nothing; the words which I have spoken to you are spirit and are life.

Col. 3:16-17 Let the word of Christ dwell in you richly. ...And whatever you do in word or in deed, do all things in the name of the Lord Jesus, giving thanks to God the Father through Him.

Date _____

Week 3 — Day 6 — Today's verses

Phil. 2:15-16 That you may be blameless and guileless, children of God without blemish in the midst of a crooked and perverted generation, among whom you shine as luminaries in the world, holding forth the word of life, so that I may have a boast in the day of Christ that I did not run in vain nor labor in vain.

Date _____

Week 3 — Day 1 — Today's verses

Col. 1:18 And He is the Head of the Body, the church; He is the beginning, the Firstborn from the dead, that He Himself might have the first place in all things.

Col. 3:16 Let the word of Christ dwell in you richly in all wisdom, teaching and admonishing one another with psalms and hymns and spiritual songs, singing with grace in your hearts to God.

Date _____

Week 3 — Day 2 — Today's verses

John 15:4 Abide in Me and I in you. As the branch cannot bear fruit of itself unless it abides in the vine, so neither can you unless you abide in Me.

7 If you abide in Me and My words abide in you, ask whatever you will, and it shall be done for you.

Date _____

Week 3 — Day 3 — Today's verses

Eph. 3:8 To me, less than the least of all saints, was this grace given to announce to the Gentiles the unsearchable riches of Christ as the gospel.

John 6:57 As the living Father has sent Me and I live because of the Father, so he who eats Me, he also shall live because of Me.

Date _____

Week 4 — Day 4

Today's verses

2 Tim. Proclaim the word; be ready in season
4:2 and out of season; convict, rebuke, exhort
with all long-suffering and teaching.

Acts Because of this I also exercise myself to
24:16 always have a conscience without offense
toward God and men.

_____
Date

Week 4 — Day 5

Today's verses

Col. Let the word of Christ dwell in you richly
3:16 in all wisdom, teaching and admonishing
one another with psalms and hymns and
spiritual songs, singing with grace in your
hearts to God.

1 Cor. What then, brothers? Whenever you
14:26 come together, each one has a psalm, has
a teaching, has a revelation, has a tongue,
has an interpretation. Let all things be
done for building up.

_____
Date

Week 4 — Day 6

Today's verses

John And the Word became flesh and taber-
1:14 nacled among us...full of grace and
reality.

Acts ...They did not cease teaching and an-
5:42 nouncing the gospel of Jesus as the Christ.

1 Cor. For to one through the Spirit a word of
12:8 wisdom is given, and to another a word of
knowledge, according to the same Spirit.

_____
Date

Week 4 — Day 1

Today's verses

Gen. And God said, Let Us make man in Our
1:26 image, according to Our likeness; and let
them have dominion...over all the earth...

Heb. God, having spoken of old in many por-
1:1-2 tions and in many ways to the fathers in
the prophets, has at the last of these days
spoken to us in the Son...

_____
Date

Week 4 — Day 2

Today's verses

Psa. My heart overflows with a good matter; I
45:1 speak what I have composed concerning
the King. My tongue is the pen of a ready
writer.

Matt. And I also say to you that you are Peter,
16:18 and upon this rock I will build My church,
and the gates of Hades shall not prevail
against it.

1 Cor. ...He who prophesies builds up the
14:4 church.

_____
Date

Week 4 — Day 3

Today's verses

1 John If we say that we have fellowship with
1:6 Him and yet walk in the darkness, we lie
and are not practicing the truth.

Psa. I anticipated the dawn and cried out; I
119:147- hoped in Your words. My eyes anticipated
148 the night watches, that I might muse upon
Your word.

_____
Date

Week 5 — Day 1

Today's verses

Acts
6:7 And the word of God grew, and the number of the disciples in Jerusalem multiplied greatly; and a large number of the priests obeyed the faith.

12:24 But the word of God grew and multiplied.

19:20 Thus, the word of the Lord grew mightily and prevailed.

Date _____

Week 5 — Day 2

Today's verses

Col.
4:3 Praying at the same time for us also, that God would open to us a door for the word, to speak the mystery of Christ…

2 Thes.
3:1 Finally, brothers, pray concerning us, that the word of the Lord may run and be glorified, even as *it is* also with you.

Acts
4:31 And when they had *so* besought, the place in which they were gathered was shaken, and they were all filled with the Holy Spirit and began to speak the word of God with boldness.

Date _____

Week 5 — Day 3

Today's verses

Heb.
5:13—6:1 For everyone who partakes of milk is inexperienced in the word of righteousness, for he is an infant; but solid food is for the full-grown, who because of practice have their faculties exercised for discriminating between both good and evil. Therefore leaving the word of the beginning of Christ, let us be brought on to maturity, not laying again a foundation of repentance from dead works and of faith in God.

Date _____

Week 5 — Day 4

Today's verses

Heb.
5:12-13 For when because of the time you ought to be teachers, you have need again for someone to teach you what the rudiments of the beginning of the oracles of God are and have become those who have need of milk and not of solid food. For everyone who partakes of milk is inexperienced in the word of righteousness…

Date _____

Week 5 — Day 5

Today's verses

2 Cor.
5:21 Him who did not know sin He made sin on our behalf that we might become the righteousness of God in Him.

2 Pet.
2:5 And did not spare the ancient world but guarded Noah, a herald of righteousness, with seven others, when He brought a flood upon the world of the ungodly.

Date _____

Week 5 — Day 6

Today's verses

Gen.
49:28 All these are the twelve tribes of Israel, and this is what their father spoke to them when he blessed them; he blessed them, each one according to his blessing.

47:7 And Joseph brought in Jacob his father and set him before Pharaoh, and Jacob blessed Pharaoh.

John
7:38 He who believes into Me, as the Scripture said, out of his innermost being shall flow rivers of living water.

Date _____